*Ghana's Political Transition
1990–1993*

GHANA'S POLITICAL TRANSITION

1990–1993

Selected Documents

Compiled with Introduction by
Kwame A. Ninsin

FREEDOM PUBLICATIONS
ACCRA
1996

Published by
Freedom Publications
P. O. Box 313
Legon, Accra
Ghana

© Kwame A. Ninsin

ALL RIGHTS RESERVED

ISBN 9964–91–595–0

Overseas Distibutors:
African Books Collective Ltd,
The Jam Factory,
27 Park End Street,
Oxford OX1 1HU,
England.

Designed and typeset at Woeli Publishing Services, Accra
Printed by Ministry of Information, Printing Department, Accra

Contents

Preface ix

Section One

DOCUMENT

Introduction 3
1. Address by the Chairman of the PNDC, Flt. Lt. Jerry John Rawlings, at the Opening Session of the Seminar for Presiding Members and Assemblymen and Women, District Secretaries, CDRs, etc., Organized by the NCD at Sunyani on Thursday, 5 July 1990 5
2. Announcement of the Formation of a Broad-Based National Movement — The Movement For Freedom and Justice (MFJ) at a Press Conference on Wednesday 1 August 1990 *Embargoed for Automatic Release on 1 August 1990 11 a.m.* 10
3. Statement by the Movement for Freedom and Justice (MFJ) on on NCD–Organized Regional Fora and a Proposed Programme on the Political Future of Ghana Accra, 28 November 1990 17
4. Statement by the National Union of Ghana Students on the Political Future of Ghana — Issued on the 4 September, 1990 23
5. Resolutions of Ghana Bar Association at its Annual Conference in Accra, 30 September to 4 October, 1990 28
6. A Memorandum to the Government of the Provisional National Defence Council from the Christian Council of Ghana on "Ghana's Search for a New Democratic System of Government" 32
7. The Catholic Church and Ghana's Search for a New Democratic System 38

Section Two

DOCUMENT

Introduction 57
8. Broadcast to the Nation by the Chairman of the PNDC, Flt-Lt Jerry John Rawlings on Tuesday, 1 January 1991 59

9. Statement of the Ghana Bar Association Made at an Emergency General Meeting of the Bar on 23 February, 1991 on the Programme for a Return to Constitutional Rule 65
10. Statement by the Movement for Freedom and Justice (MFJ) on the New Year Broadcast of the PNDC Chairman and other Related Matters at a Press Conference in Accra, 11 January 1991 69
11. Evolving a True Democracy: Summary of Memoranda Submitted to the NCD 76
12. Executive Summary Regional Seminar on "District Assemblies and the Evolving Democratic Process" 80
13. Government's Statement on the NCD Report on Evolving True Democracy 99
14. Statement by the Movement for Freedom and Justice (MFJ) on the PNDC'S Statement on the "NCD Report and the Constitutional Proposals" Accra, 17, May 1991 103
15. Ghana Bar Association Statement on the Return to Constitutional Rule 111
16. Statement of the Ghana Bar Association Made at an Emergency General Meeting of the Bar on Saturday 11 May 1991 on the NCD Report and the PNDC's Statement on the Said Report 113
17. Memorandum from the Heads of the Member Churches of the Christian Council of Ghana and the Catholic Bishops' Conference on the Release of the Report on the Evolving Democratic Process 117
18. The Inaugural Address on the Occasion of the First Session of the Consultative Assembly by Flt.-Lt. J. J. Rawlings, Chairman of the PNDC. and Head of State, 26 August 1991 118

Section Three

DOCUMENT

Introduction 129
19. NUGS Statement on the PNDC's Time Table on the Return to Constitutional Rule 132
20. Statement by the Ghana Bar Association on the Transitional Provisions of the Constitution 134
21. Statement by the Ghana Bar Association on the PNDC's Transitional Programme 137

22. National Union of Ghana Students Statement
on the Transitional Provisions of the Constitution 141
23. Statement by the Ghana Bar Association on the
Draft Constitution of the Republic of Ghana
and the Proposed Referendum Thereon..........................143
24. Political Parties Law 1992 (PNDC Law 281) (Excerpts).........147
25. Ghana Bar Association Press Conference
Need For a Transitional Government 152
26. Ghana Bar Association 1991/92 Annual Conference
Held at Sekondi/Takoradi from 5 to 8 October, 1992
Resolution No. 16/1992 Register of Voters......................156
27. Ghana Bar Association 1991/1992 Annual Conference Held
at Sekondi/Takoradi from 5 October to 8 October 1992
Resolution No. . 17 /1992
Matters Affecting the Nation..158
28. Memorandum from the Christian Council of Ghana and the
Catholic Church to the Interim Electoral Commission 162
29. The National Union of Ghana Students(NUGS) Resolution
Declaring a Boycott of the 29 December Parliamentary
Elections 165
30. Statement by Ghana Bar Association on the Promulgation
of the Constitution of the Fourth Republ ic 167

Appendices

*Selected Documents Expressing the Political Position of the
Ghana Trades Union Congress During the Late 1980s*

A. "The Trade Unions and Democracy in Ghana" Paper
Presented to the National Commission on Democracy by
the Trades Union Congress 171
B. Extract from Secretary General's May Day
Address, 1987...175
C. Resolutions Adopted by the 3rd Quadrennial Delegates
Congress of the Trade Union Congress (Ghana) Held at the
University of Cape Coast from 16 to 18 March, 1988............176

22. National Union of Ghana Students Statement
    on the Transitional Provisions of the Constitution 141
23. Statement by the Ghana Bar Association on the
    Draft Constitution of the Republic of Ghana
    and the Proposed Referendum thereon 143
24. Political Parties Law 1992 (PNDC Law 281) (Excerpts) 147
25. Ghana Bar Association Press Conference:
    Need for a Transitional Government 152
26. Ghana Bar Association, 1991/92 Annual Conference
    Held at Sefwedi, Takoradi from 5 to 8 October, 1992
    Resolution No. 16, 1992 Register of Voters 156
27. Ghana Bar Association 1991/1992 Annual Conference Held
    at Sefwedi, Takoradi from 5 October to 8 October 1992
    Resolution No. 17, 1992 ....
    Military Attacks on the Judiciary 158
28. Memorandum from the Christian Council of Ghana and the
    Catholic Church to the Interim National Commission 162
29. The National Union of Ghana Students (NUGS) Resolution
    Meeting held out of the 29 December Parliamentary
    Election 168
30. Statement of the Ghana Bar Association at its Extraordinary
    on the Elections and the January Institutes 169

Appendices

A. The Trades Unions and Democracy in Ghana: Paper
   Presented to the National Congress of Trade Unions by
   the Trades Union Congress, Ghana 171
B. Extract from Speeches Quoted, May 1992 ....
   Addendum 195
C. Resolutions Adopted by the Parliamentary Delegation
   Conference of the Bar Cultural Congress Ghana, Held at the
   University of Cape Coast from 14 to 16 March, 1998 206

Preface

In November–December of 1992 presidential and parliamentary elections were held to choose a new government for Ghana under a new constitution which had been approved at a referendum held on 28 April of the same year. Then on 7 January the new government took office under President Jerry John Rawlings. Ghana's Fourth Republic was born on this day, an important landmark in the country's successive attempts to institutionalize a democratic order.

These events terminated the life of the military regime, the Provisional National Defence Council (PNDC) of J. J. Rawlings which had seized power from a democratically-elected government on 31 December, 1981. The events also represented the glorious fruits of years of struggle against that military government and for the restoration of constitutional democratic rule. The truth of the matter is that those struggles were initiated in the first few months of the life of the PNDC government. However, it was from 1990 that a conjuncture of events, largely domestic, precipitated what has been generally described as a transition to democracy. At its peak the struggle for democracy involved an assortment of social forces acting, often individually and often in concert, to oppose the military government. As often happens, the actors in political struggles used the power of the print media effectively to supplement other actions as a means of legitimizing their positions, mobilizing public opinion and propelling their struggle forward.

This volume brings together key documents in the politics of the transition to democracy in Ghana. On the one hand, they represent the critical positions of the military government, the PNDC, as it increasingly came under pressure from the social forces that were most active in the pro-democracy movement. On the other hand, they sum up the unyielding demands of the major social forces that were engaged in the pro-democracy movement. I chose January 1990 to January 1993 as the parameter within which to highlight these struggles for two reasons. First, 1990 could be legitimately considered as the watershed in the transition politics. It marked the historic moment when the social forces engaged in the pro-democracy movement gained that critical mass which alone could propel the transition on to an irreversible path. Second, without implying that the inauguration of a democratically-elected government constitutes the highest point of democratic politics, January 1993 nonetheless is a historic date in the history of democratic politics in Ghana.

On that date, 7 January, 1993 to be precise, the military regime of the PNDC fell; it was replaced by a metamorphosed version of itself. But henceforth that remnant of the military regime would be compelled by the sovereign politics of the people to learn to live by the letter and spirit of the 1992 Constitution under which it had come to power.

In the heat of the transition politics, the documents which expressed the demands of the pro-democracy forces were disseminated as widely as possible, often through very informal channels. Of course, statements by the government were widely publicized through the state media and could be found lodged in libraries. But the statements of the pro-democracy social forces did not enjoy this advantage and so stood the chance of being lost to history. This collection is intended to bring to the attention of generations today and tomorrow some of the historic documents which have shaped the course of Ghana's recent political history.

The following criteria were used to select the documents which have been reproduced here.

(i) How important a documents is and

(ii) how influential it was in those historic moments.

A document was judged *important* and *influential* if the social forces which were its source were engaged in sustained struggle with the military regime to back up their expressed demands in such a document. This elaboration is important because the politics of transition, being a struggle against a dictatorial or authoritarian regime, is liberatory and potentially revolutionary politics. The agents of social liberation should therefore be seen in active combat against the forces of oppression. In such circumstances mere pamphleteering is of little or no consequence.

In using these criteria therefore, I was obliged to exclude a large collection of very interesting and often powerful memoranda which the National Commission for Democracy (NCD), for example, had received from individuals and groups of the Ghanaian public during the long period of its search for a democratic alternative. These are still available in the library of the National Commission for Civic Education (NCCE), and open to the public.

These criteria notwithstanding, the problem of access to public documents in general was compounded by the swift current of the politics of struggle. As a result, it was impossible to include several other vital documents. A good example of this unitentional omission is the set of position papers published by the Ghana Trades Union Congress (TUC) during the 1990–93 period. During the research for this publication, I sought in vain for access to such documents which I am sure would have enriched the present collection. To make up for this loss, and also reveal the extent of the labour movement's political perspectives during those critical moments, I have reproduced in the appendix a set of documents which was published in the late 1980s. I hope that people who have responsibility for collecting and storing vital public documents such as these would avert the recurrence of such regrettable losses by cultivating and maintaining a culture of conscientious duty.

The collection is divided into three sections. Each section is preceded by a brief introduction which is intended to place the various documents in the appropriate conjuncture when the issues of freedom and democracy were placed irrevocably on the nation's political agenda. The introductions should not be mistaken for commentaries. Readers are expected to derive their own conclusions from the documents.

In the final preparation of this publication, I have enjoyed the generous advice and assistance of a number of people. Some of these innocently gave encouraging words. Others were more forthright. I thank all of such noble souls. I should register special appreciation for the person who patiently and efficiently typed the manuscript, Godfried Mantey of the Department of Political Science at Legon. But for his devoted service, this project would have suffered incalculable delay.

KWAME A. NINSIN
Department of Political Science
University of Ghana, Legon

Section One
1990–1993

Section One
1990–1993

Introduction

On 1 July 1987 the government of the Provisional National Defence Council (PNDC) published a document entitled *District Political Authority and Modalities for District Level Elections*. "The Blue Book", as it came to be called, outlines the government's philosophy and policy on future political reforms for the country. It laid out a decentralized system of government in which the District Assembly would be the highest political authority. Apart from this there were two features of the reforms that are noteworthy: (i) Election to the district assemblies was to be non-partisan; (ii) the District Assemblies would form the basis for any future representative institutions that would emerge at the national level.

These two elements of the proposed reforms immediately revealed the government's political agenda which contradicted the demands of the pro-democracy forces then actively engaged in a struggle against the PNDC government. In other words, it was evident that the PNDC government was not prepared to allow multi-party politics. Nor was it prepared to see the formation of a national government based on popular elections. The implications of the PNDC's position for the demand for a return to liberal democracy were too clear to be ignored. It meant, for example, that the democratic political rights and freedoms of association, opinion, speech or expression, assembly as well as the key democratic credo of government by consent could not be realized under the PNDC's reforms. The outcome of the district assembly elections held in 1988/89 under the Local Government Law 1988 (PNDCL 207), under which 30% of the members of the proposed district assemblies would be nominated by the government, confirmed this view.

Meanwhile the government had intensified its repressive actions against its critics and the opposition. There were arbitrary arrests, detentions without trial, and other repressive actions. The government proceeded to reopen the voters' register, and formed public education and election committees despite widespread demonstrations. These and other developments convinced the pro-democracy forces of the fact that the government was least prepared to initiate the necessary reforms towards a democratic order.

The pro-democracy forces did not take this lying down. They intensified their criticism. The 1988 J. B. Danquah Memorial Lectures delivered in February of that year by Professor Albert Adu-Boahen opened a new wave of criticism and agitations for democratic reforms. In March of the same year, the Ghana Trades Union Congress (TUC) held its Third Quadrennial Delegates Congress at the end of which it issued a communique calling on the government to respect the fundamental rights of Ghanaians and further convene a constitutional conference to write a new constitution for the country. This was closely followed in May by a similar statement issued by the National Union of Ghana Students (NUGS) at the end of its annual congress imploring the government to, among other things, repeal all repressive laws and restore constitutional rule.

It was against this background of escalating public criticism and agitation that the PNDC government conducted the district assembly election in 1988/89 under the Local Government Law 1988 (PNDCL 207). Furthermore the Head of State, J. J. Rawlings, inaugurated the first regional forum on the theme "The District Assemblies and the Evolving Democratic Process". It was clear from Rawlings' inaugural address, and the political character of the audience at that and subsequent regional fora that the PNDC government had not abandoned its intention to impose its own "democratic" regime on the people of Ghana.

The formation of the Movement for Freedom and Justice must be understood against this background of a military regime that was resolved to defy the legitimate demands and aspirations of a people waking up from several years of oppression. The unprecedented acts of mobilization by the leadership of the Christian Council of Ghana and the Catholic Bishops Conference of their respective congregations throughout the country for periods of prayer and intervention in the transition stalemate with a view to pushing the country's politics in a democratic direction should also be read against the background of those dramatic developments. In any case, the transition politics of the country had by then reached a point where the only option was movement forward.

DOCUMENT 1

Address by the Chairman of the PNDC, Flt. Lt. Jerry John Rawlings, at the Opening Session of the Seminar for Presiding Members and Assemblymen and Women, District Secretaries, CDRs, etc., Organized by the NCD at Sunyani on Thursday, 5 July 1990

[ ]At the beginning of this week, on 1 July, 1990 we commemorated thirty years of being a Republic and, quite naturally, as we ponder the last three decades, we will be looking ahead to what the future holds. As I indicated early this year, the intention of the PNDC is to intensify the process of national consultations with a view to taking steps towards the building up of our national democratic future. The overall theme of the seminars —"The District Assemblies and the Evolving Democratic Process", aptly expresses the importance that we all attach to the District Assemblies in the evolution of the new democracy.

The District Assemblies have been in place for just about a year and a half, but we can already see from their work a developing sense of responsibility and the pride and confidence in being a part of a new-found political vitality. Much of the crippling apathy and helplessness which had overwhelmed most Ghanaians over the past decade is being overcome. The role that Committees for the Defence of the Revolution and other revolutionary organs have also been playing in bringing about this new atmosphere is also worthy of note and I must pay my respects to all those whose steadfast and conscientious work is creating such beneficial changes in attitudes in our country.

Admittedly, as with every new approach, there have been some teething problems; and sadly, some of these problems arise because some of us are still steeped in the old ways of "politics", and we see our positions as entitling us to order everybody around and to be more concerned about status than about service. These unfortunate attitudes have to be put behind us so that we can all work together to achieve the historic objectives we have set.

From the beginning of the 31st December Revolution, indeed since the June 4th Uprising, our aim has been to establish a true democracy in which ordinary Ghanaians participate meaningfully in the processes through which they are governed. And that is why we must soon compliment (*sic*) the work of the District Assemblies with the structures at Town and Area levels and even further down to the unit structures.

[ ] In order to achieve a close touch with our representatives and the community, we departed from the old practice enshrined in the previous Constitution whereby, for instance, the English language became a barrier to the capacity of many wise and able people to represent our interest in [ ] the Assemblies. The large majority of the citizens of Ghana do not read and write the English language even if it is a convenient language of national administration and international communication. We could not therefore pretend that only those who could read and write English should effectively represent the people. What we insisted upon was simply that, candidates present themselves before their own people to be judged on their own merit.

It is the firm view of the PNDC that both national productivity as well as the effectiveness of political authority in our country depend on the strength of popular participation. Indeed, we have found it unacceptable that in the past, the productive majority of our country were denied real participation in the political system through various means.

First of all, so much mystery was made to surround the holding of political office that accountability to the people was out of the question. Thus, elected representatives interacted very little with those they were supposed to represent so as to know their problems and help solve them. Being elected to "Assembly" in the past, became a passport out of one's humble origins to a new lifestyle in the cities such as Accra. But now we are locating the "Assembly" where it really belongs — with the communities — and we expect Assemblymen and women to maintain constant touch with their constituents, (*sic*) to know and feel their problems and to be with them in finding solutions. It is one thing to know a problem in your head, but to feel it and be part of the solution requires another kind of human passion.

But let us make no mistake: Some people do not like this proper approach to democracy, with its insistence on the participation of the ordinary people. To them, ordinary people do not understand politics and cannot participate in any process of government. But we know from our nation's history that our very independence and nationhood owed everything to the determined struggle of ordinary farmers, ordinary workers, ordinary soldiers, ex-servicemen — who were all often barely educated and yet were prepared to lay down their lives to win for us the dignity of being Ghanaian.

There are those who would prefer to restore themselves and their personal and factional interests to power and are therefore not happy about the District Assemblies as the cornerstone of our democratic future, and they will do everything to undermine these foundations. But [ ] we must stand firm together in the service of our people so that the processes we have initiated are not toyed with or hijacked, so that democracy can become a living reality.

[ ] The high turnout of over 60% of registered voters contrasts with the less than 40% in the 1979 elections. Even in Accra where 44% of the voters turned up, this was a marked improvement on the figure of only 18% in 1979. During the platforms mounted by the candidates, we saw for the first time the spontaneous and vibrant participation in this new approach to establishing real democracy. No objective observer of those elections can doubt our commitment to a free and fair electoral process. But I must emphasize that our commitment is to an electoral process that will deliver the goods and not just a mechanical ritual as had been happening in the past.

For us, democracy cannot simply mean holding District Assembly elections or any other elections periodically whilst we continue to endure poverty, misery, illiteracy, hunger and poor health facilities and whilst many of our able-bodied citizens are unable to find employment.

We cannot divorce any discussion on structures or processes of government from the economic reality of providing [ ] basic human needs for society. And even as we focus attention on resolving the practical concerns of the District Assemblies, it is important to consider, alongside, the need to accelerate national discussion on the structure of government that will tie the District Assemblies within the constituted arrangements for the evolving democratic system.

But to begin with, it must be recognized that our democratic ideals can only be realized within a stable and viable economy which provides opportunities for each and everyone. As I have previously emphasized, a national consensus is needed on how to build such a viable economy capable of providing basic necessities affordable by the people.

The record of the PNDC in responding to the grave crisis of the national economy and the modest results which have been registered in the recovery of the economy can only be sustained into the future if we establish a framework that ensures fair reward for productivity instead of allowing a few to benefit unjustly from the work of the majority. In societies such as ours, where for the vast majority even survival is a struggle, the sheer greed of those who only see opportunities for personal luxury and feel no responsibility for contributing to the overall welfare has been one of the major obstacles to our progress.

You all know that Ghana is a country with tremendous resources that can provide wealth and satisfaction to all of us if we can each put in our quota towards the sustained health of the economy. And that is why we have emphasized the need for a national consensus about the economy; a consensus which will be the basis upon which the economy will have to be built in the future by every administration. Elected or appointed persons, including us, may come and go but the health of the economy and its progression will have to remain the same.

No framework for our economic and political future can ignore the international situation and our responsibilities for the attainment of a new international economic relationship. Most of the manifestations of political instability in many developing countries today can be traced to poverty and inequality much of which have roots in colonialism and the present unjust world economic system. Freedom and justice stand little chance in a world of such pronounced inequalities and it is thoughtless to speak about political reforms without paying attention to the economic justice that will make such reforms meaningful.

The seriousness of the plight of developing countries has been well summarized in a recent survey on World Economic Trends published very recently (May) by the International Monetary Fund (IMF). We are told that in 1986 alone, the income gain to the seven major industrial countries (that is, the United States, Britain, France, Germany, Japan, Canada and Italy) through paying low prices for our commodities was equivalent to 115 billion dollars. This enabled the citizens of those countries to avoid the sharp increases in the cost of living in that period that we (you and I) suffered. The report, obviously written by those who are not feeling the heat of the fire that we are in, mildly describes how the adverse trends in the international economy damaged the growth of the developing countries, but it interestingly concludes: "the absence of major adverse price shocks in the industrial countries also benefitted the developing countries through a generally steady expansion in the volume of world trade". What logic!

This so-called benefit to developing countries consisted of the millions of infants who died before they were five years of age. It also consisted of the death in childbirth of many mothers. However, in the developed countries maternal mortality rates rarely exceed 20 for every 100,000 live births, but in our situation there are often 1,000 or more mothers dying for every 100,000 live births. These are our benefits from the so-called stable economic environment of the 1980s in which seven countries gained 115 billion dollars in one year alone at our expense. [ ] Even if we should take away a few too many unplanned and unaffordable births, it will not make any difference. [ ] Despite these adverse international conditions which threaten our basic freedom — freedom from want — we will not be deterred from pursuing our goals of evolving democratic national institutions. When everything is taken away, our dignity cannot be taken away.

The Revolution launched on 31st December 1981 has reinforced our commitment to the national motto of Freedom and Justice and insisted that these principles can only be realized where there is accountability to the people. The PNDC has already stated that the evolution of new democratic institutions must involve the active participation of all Ghanaians. And I trust that this effort by the NCD to organize a series of discussions on the evolving democratic structures will move us closer to our objective of a new political order. Our democratic institutions will have to satisfy the aspirations and yearnings of Ghanaians. The content of the structures we aim at should make democracy a daily reality. It is not simply a matter of abstract ideas written into a constitutional document. We must remember that constitutions are made to live and not just written to stay on paper. Therefore let us turn our minds during the next few months to a common effort to hammer out some specific ideas and proposals that will yield a collective picture of our future [to] which all true patriots will be proud to pledge their loyalty and commitment. We must harness to the fullest the whole range of human resources and place them at the disposal of the country. And in this connection, I must point out that the skills and manpower resources of the military and other security services will need to be effectively integrated into that collective picture. We must also underline the importance of maintaining national unity and promoting reconciliation within the fabric of our nation.

[ ] When we look back over the experiences of the 1st, 2nd and 3rd Republics, it is clear that our attempts at establishing democratic national institutions failed because fragile super-structures were created without a firm base. That lesson imposes on us the duty this time to build a solid foundation and ensure that the institutions of central government are rooted in these firm foundations. A lot will have to be made to ensure that the foundations we lay will be very firm for the improvement in the lives of the people in their constituencies.

[ ] The key to our evolving democratic system lies in ordinary people feeling capable of acting on their own behalf. With lessons of three failed constitutions, our aim is to establish a new constitutional framework that will be based on a firm foundation; it must be a house built upon the rock and not upon sand, because we know that even a breeze is all it takes to bring down the house that is built on mere sand.

You all have an important role in laying these firm foundations and I hope, over the next few months we can intensify our consultations and thereby arrive at the framework for a stable and lasting constitutional order.

DOCUMENT 2

Announcement of the Formation of a Broad-Based National Movement — The Movement For Freedom and Justice (MFJ) at a Press Conference on Wednesday 1 August 1990

Embargoed for Automatic Release on 1 August 1990 11 a.m.

[ ] We have invited you here this morning to announce through you to the people of Ghana and the international community the formation of a broad and open nation-wide movement to campaign for the restoration of democratic rule in our country. We shall in the course of this conference also outline the reasons for our historic move, make known the aims and objectives of the movement, proclaim its slogans and introduce its principal interim officers.

Our movement, formed by a group of public inspirited *(sic)* Ghanaian men and women representing the whole spectrum of political, ideological and religious persuasions and from different social, class, occupational and ethnic background has been named MOVEMENT FOR FREEDOM AND JUSTICE (MFJ).

We ask and demand that our movement should be given the same chance and opportunities as are accorded the 31st December Women's Movement, the June Four Movement and other organizations associated with the government which are free to organize and advance their objectives through a free access to the mass media and without state security harassment and repression.

The formation of the MFJ has been precipitated by a number of considerations. The first and most important is, of course, the inauguration of the national debate on the future political structure for the country. While we welcome this initiative on the part of the PNDC, we cannot but express our profound dissatisfaction with the manner in which it has been conducted so far. Naturally, every debate or discussion, if it is real, cannot foreclose the possibility of opposing views. Unfortunately the current debate has been confined to only those individuals and groups in favour of the positions officially or unofficially adopted by the PNDC.

While it is true that the PNDC has proclaimed officially that it has not decided on any type of political system for the country, it is nonetheless obvious to even the most simple-minded person that the PNDC is at least opposed to the multi-party system. How else can one explain the overwhelming prominence being given to arguments against the multi-party system in the government-controlled mass media? Clearly the debate has been one-sided against all the norms of justice and the democratic process of arriving at decisions and consensus.

The atmosphere in which the debate is being conducted is also agonizing and reprehensible. We wonder how any serious, meaningful and objective national debate can be conducted in the face of the suffocating control of the mass media by the PNDC and the existence of the obnoxious Newspaper Licensing Law (PNDC Law 211). The distortion of recent statements issued by the Catholic Bishops Conference and the Kwame Nkrumah Revolutionary Guards (KNRG), by the "People's Daily Graphic" and the fact that other media houses completely ignored them, should convince all and sundry of the helplessness and hopelessness of the state of the Ghana mass media today. We of the MFJ believe that the local MASS MEDIA SHOULD BE LIBERATED FROM THE GRIP OF THE PNDC.

Secondly, the atmosphere of fear, suspicion and intimidation and the existence of the culture of silence caused by the ready application of such oppressive laws as the Preventive Custody Law cannot make for a free and fair debate.

Thirdly, the government has not come out with a programme which clearly sets out the character and duration of the national debate and the mechanism for determining its outcome. This way, it would appear that the government would be free at any time to produce any position as the national consensus as it did in relation to the "debate" on its Educational Reform Programme and the District Assembly concept.

Finally, we consider as highly dangerous to the political health of our country and to the national development effort that decisions affecting a whole country are not subject to the will of the people and that a group of individuals who have no mandate and are accountable to no one wields the powers of government and is free to take policy decisions in the name of the people.

It is in the light of the above stated considerations that we have decided to take the challenging step of coming together to form the MOVEMENT FOR FREEDOM AND JUSTICE to bring together all Ghanaians of whatever walk of life, who believe that the future of Ghana is a question that can be determined only by all Ghanaians.

[ ] Before we go on to declare the aims and objectives of the MFJ,

we would like to react to some of the arguments that have so far been advanced against the multi-party system. Supporters of the status quo have said that the multi-party system is being imposed on the country by foreign interests, that it breeds corruption, and that it provokes tribalism, violence, animosity and polarization. They also insist that a sound economic base needs to be established before thought is given to democracy based on the multi-party system. All these arguments, are mere red-herring, for the multi-party system is not just concerned with the freedom to form parties, it provides the political framework for ensuring that in the art of public life and government the fundamental rights of the people including the right of free expression, association, personal security and worship are guaranteed.

The claim that the multi-party system is an imposition on African countries by the western powers is to say the least ridiculous having regard to the fact that the history of Ghana even in the colonial era is the history of struggles for basic freedoms and multi-party democracy. Even since the PNDC came to power through the barrel of the gun rather than the ballot box and especially within the last five years or so, various bodies such the Ghana Bar Association, the National Union of Ghana Students, the Catholic Secretariat, the New Democratic Movement and the Kwame Nkrumah Revolutionary Guards have persistently demanded the restoration of the multi-party system of government.

In February 1988, that is two years before the phenomenal and revolutionary events that erupted in Eastern Europe and well before external pressure was mounted on the PNDC to democratize Ghanaian society, the lecturer at a well patronized public lecture vigorously advocated the multi-party system of government for Ghana.

The argument that multi-party democracy provokes tribalism was clearly disproved during the last civilian elections, thanks to the clause in the constitution which insisted that only parties with substantial support in all the regions of the country were to be registered by the Electoral Commissioner. There is no reason why this wise provision should not be retained in any future constitution. Similarly, though the multi-party system of government can breed corruption because of the demands of those who finance them, the way out is surely not the retention of military dictatorships, not no-party or one-party systems. The solution lies in the financing of political parties and their electoral campaigns by the state. Besides, it must be recognized that the coups that bring to power military dictatorships are themselves financed often by big businessmen and politicians, sometimes even by foreign interests.

Furthermore, we consider the suggestion that the district assemblies be used to constitute structures of government at the national level(s) a fraud and an imposition. For though the principle of local and district level structures of government is laudable, the current district assembly structures are vitiated by a number of undemocratic characteristics they possess. First, the district assemblies were imposed on the people of this country without any real discussion and the consent of the people. Nor can the composition of the assemblies be said to be democratic considering the fact that one-third of their members are appointed by the PNDC. Further, the head of the district executive, the most powerful office in the system, is the District Secretary who is a PNDC appointee. The district assemblies themselves are severely restricted in their deliberations by PNDC Law 207 and have no legally recognized means of contributing to national policy formulation. On the contrary, they simply implement national policies and decrees dictated by the PNDC. For all these reasons, we can safely say the district assemblies, are not a true expression of the democratic will of Ghanaians and therefore cannot be used as the basis for the development of the future national political system of our country.

Finally, the contention that we need to have a sound economic base before the restoration of political pluralism only betrays the undemocratic character of those who push it. Perhaps they imagine that politics can be separated from economics and that the people can be excluded from the choice of economic arrangements that will facilitate the establishment of the solid base. We dare also ask when a country can be said to have laid a solid economic base, and what country in the world today has managed to solve all its economic problems. Are the developed countries of the North not still plagued by problems of budget deficits, inflation and unemployment? In any case what is politics about if not the solution of economic and social problems? To ask for the solution of economic problems before the restoration of multi-party democracy is in our view tantamount to putting the cart before the horse.

Certainly, we do recognize that there have been many undemocratic practices and other problems inimical to the country's welfare and progress during periods of multi-party rule in our country, but we also want to state emphatically that these same problems are not limited to multi-party rule. Indeed during periods of no-party rule, the basic rights of the people tend to be trampled upon even more, while there is every evidence to prove that it has been relatively easier for ordinary people to express their views publicly about violations of their rights under multi-party rule.

It is our view then that the multi-party system of government will provide a better atmosphere for all Ghanaians whether individuals or more, especially through their mass organizations to express their views and defend their rights without arbitrary government interference. A multi-party arrangement which is not imposed on the people, and which is not constrained by laws and social forces opposed to open democratic expression, has a better chance of ensuring genuine probity and accountability under the rule of law. It provides a more democratic mechanism for involving all the people in coming to grips with the economic problems facing the country.

We are, on our part, deeply convinced that *only a political system that guarantees the fundamental human rights and political liberties of the people, that enables people of like-minded views freely to associate, and form political parties to contest office, and in which the people elect their own leaders through free and fair elections can be considered truly democratic.* That is what the multi-party system is all about.

In the final analysis, our view is that whether or not the people of Ghana want the multi-party system of government is a matter to be decided by the people themselves. It is gratifying in this regard that the Chairman of the PNDC has assured Ghanaians and the world that he will not stand in the way of Ghanaians if they want multi-party democracy restored. *The only way to find out what the true views and feeling of the people are is through a genuine* national debate culminating in a NATIONAL REFERENDUM organized by an independent body.

Under the existing political climate of the country, however, it is neither possible to ascertain what Ghanaians truly think about the future political system of our country nor arrive at a national consensus on this vital question. In order to create an atmosphere which permits and guarantees free and open national discussion of the country's political future, we demand the repeal of all repressive laws, especially:

The Preventive Custody Law, (PNDC Law 4)
The Habeas Corpus Amendment Law, (PNDC Law 91)
The Newspaper Licensing Law (PNDC Law 211)
The sections of the Public Tribunal Law PNDC Law 78 which deal with executions for political offences.

We also call for the release of all political prisoners and detainees and unconditional amnesty for all political exiles. [ ] We now state (in detail) the aims and objectives of the MFJ. They are:

1. To work for the restoration of multi-party democracy and civilian rule in Ghana.
2. To fight for the recognition and realization of the fundamental human and democratic rights of the people of Ghana to decide how they shall be governed and to choose their own leaders

through free and fair elections at both national and local levels.
3. To uphold the sovereignty of the people of Ghana.
4. To uphold and defend the democratic and human rights of the people, including the freedom of expression, especially of the press, freedom of association, freedom of worship, universal adult suffrage and the rule of law.
5. To fight against all forms of dictatorship and domination.
6. To serve as a vehicle for the mobilization of the people to carry out activities designed to lead to the establishment of democratic rule in Ghana.
7. To contribute to the development of a culture of democracy in Ghana.
8. To support people in other African countries fighting for democratic government.
9. To organize such other activities that will contribute to the realization of the objectives stated [ ].

In pursuit of the ideals we stand for, we have adopted the following slogans:

TRUE DEMOCRACY — NOW!
FREEDOM — JUSTICE
MFJ — TOWARDS THE FOURTH REPUBLIC!!!

Our interim principal officers are:

Chairman — Professor Adu Boahen
1st Vice Chairman — Johnny Hansen
2nd Vice Chairman — Ray Kakraba Quarshie
National Secretary — Obeng Manu
Deputy National Secretary — Kwesi Pratt, Jnr.
National Organizer — John Ndebugre
National Treasurer — Dan Lartey.

In conclusion, we would like to observe that in forming this movement and making this public statement, we are only exercising our sovereign right and living up to our responsibilities as citizens of Ghana to participate in the public affairs of our country and to express our views and convictions. There is absolutely nothing subversive about this. On the contrary, it is to the health of our country's polity. Ours is an open, public and above-board movement. Our activities will constantly be in the full glare of the public for the people to judge. We therefore call on the good people of Ghana to join the MOVEMENT FOR FREEDOM AND JUSTICE (MFJ). We are convinced that if you join us, together we can work for the restoration of democratic rule in our country. We urge you all to join us today to demand a broad, open and free national discussion of Ghana's political future; join us to demand a NATIONAL REFERENDUM organized by an independent body to decide what political system the people want for the country; join us to campaign for the restoration of multi-party democracy in our country. [ ]

Signed by:
Prof. Adu Boahen
(Chairman)

Obeng Manu
(National Secretary)

Johnny F.S. Hansen
(1st Vice Chairman)

Kwesi Pratt, Jnr.
(Deputy National Secretary)

Dan Lartey
(National Treasurer)

A. Owusu Gyimah
(Executive Member)

John Ndebugre
(National Organizer)

Akoto Ampaw
(Executive Member)

DOCUMENT 3

Statement by the Movement for Freedom and Justice (MFJ) on the NCD–Organized Regional Fora and a Proposed Programme on the Political Future of Ghana Accra, 28 November 1990

It is three weeks since the regional fora organized by the PNDC's National Commission for Democracy (NCD) on the political future of the country came to an end, and Ghanaians must begin to look ahead to the next stages in the process of establishing a democratic system of government in the country.

Through this press conference, the Movement for Freedom and Justice (MFJ) wishes to present to the people of Ghana and the world community what it believes to be the objective conclusions that must be drawn from the deliberations at these fora, and also what, in its view, should be the subsequent phases in the process of establishing democratic government in Ghana. In doing this, we are only exercising our right as Ghanaians to express our views on important matters of public life affecting the destiny of our country.

We note with regret that despite repeated calls by several independent organizations for the repeal of a number of repressive laws — PNDC Law 4, Law 91, Law 211, Law 221, and sections of Law 78 dealing with executions for political offences — so as to create the political atmosphere conducive to genuine national debate and free expression, the PNDC has maintained a disturbing silence over these popular and elementary democratic demands. We are therefore reiterating our call for the immediate repeal of all these oppressive laws as well as for the release of all political prisoners and detainees and an unconditional amnesty for all political exiles. These democratic demands must be met before any further steps are taken towards establishing a democratic political system for the country.

On the substantive issue of what system of government Ghanaians want, there can be no doubt that the *only objective conclusion that can be drawn from the discussions at the fora is that there are two fundamentally opposing viewpoints: the viewpoint of multi-party democracy, based on fundamental human rights and political pluralism on the one hand, and, on the other, the viewpoint of the no-party system, whose advocates do not seem to consider the question of human rights and political freedom relevant to the political future of the country.*

We notice with disquiet however that, notwithstanding these two opposing positions, the Vice Chairman of the PNDC and Chairman of the NCD, Justice Francis Daniel Annan, chose to proclaim at the close of the Wa forum that "the multi-party system has woefully failed the people (of Ghana) despite the several chances accorded that system". This prophetic statement is not only historically incorrect, but clearly indicates that, despite the repeated denials by the PNDC that it has no pre-termined position on the political future of the country, the Chairman of the NCD has already excluded (sic) the multi-party system of politics for Ghana. *As a matter of principle, this disqualifies the honourable PNDC member from playing the impartial role expected of him as chairman of the NCD, and once again vindicates the demand that the NCD should be replaced by an independent body which is not subordinated to the PNDC, if Ghanaians are to have any faith in the whole exercise.*

It must be stated very clearly that since two distinct and opposing views have emerged in the course of the discussions, any attempt to decree a no-party system as the "national consensus" would be dangerous for the political health of the country. On the other hand, it is quite obvious that the overwhelming majority of Ghanaians, excepting PNDC agents and supporters, are opposed to the no-party system, for they know from their own historical experience that the no-party system is in fact a one-party system and only breeds dictatorship, arbitrariness and arrogance in politics. The opposition of Ghanaians to the no-party system was eloquently demonstrated just thirteen years ago when the whole country totally rejected Acheampong's "union government" policy. It is therefore not necessary to take the country through that ordeal again.

This view is further strengthened by the fact that throughout the NCD regional fora, not a single independent mass or professional organization expressed views in support of the no-party system. On the contrary, all the major non-governmental organizations and bodies — the TUC, the GNAT, the Ghana Registered Nurses Association, the NUGS, the Ghana Medical Association, the Ghana Bar Association — have taken positions for multi-party democracy. In addition, though the Catholic Bishops' Conference and the Christian Council of Ghana did not take part in the fora, their repeated calls for multi-party democracy and respect for fundamental human rights are well known. It ought then to be obvious that, in the main, only government loyalists and organs of rule, such as the district assemblies and [the] likes, have come out in support of the no-party system. Their views however cannot be given much weight since these agents and bodies of the PNDC government have a stake in the present no-party system and cannot but speak from the standpoint of their self-interest. We recall, in this regard, that one assemblyman at the Volta regional forum let the cat out of the bag when he said that "now that they have tasted power" they were not going to relinquish it.

If in the fact of this overwhelming support for multi-party democracy the PNDC still insists on the no-party system as a credible political option, then it can have no alternative but to put the question whether Ghanaians want multi-party democracy or a no-party system to the acid test of *a national referendum, organized by an independent electoral body and not by the PNDC's NCD*. Any attempt to decree unilaterally a no-party system as the "national consensus" would be nothing but an imposition and will meet the massive resistance of the people of this country.

Before presenting our perspectives on what the programme for the establishment of democratic rule in the country should be, we find it necessary to comment on a number of views that have emerged in the course of the discussions at the fora.

The view that advocates multi-party democracy as opposed to a system of local government, whether it is called district assemblies or district councils, is simply groundless. There is absolutely nothing in the nature of multi-party democracy that is incompatible with local and district level structures of government, and we wish to reiterate our position that "a strong local government system is an important foundation for democratic government". The important principle of election of all representatives of the people must however be upheld.

There have also been contributions, especially by high state officials to the effect that constitutions in themselves do not ensure democracy. This, in our view, is self-evident. In the final analysis, what is decisive is the way the people, especially the leading political actors and those who hold the sacred trust of office, conduct themselves in the political arena and strive to make the constitution a living political reality. It appears however that members of the PNDC government have jumped from the legitimate caution that a constitution in itself does not settle the question of democracy to the completely erroneous conclusion that a democratic constitution is of no relevance to our present attempt at developing a culture of democracy and building democratic institutions. We are of the opinion that this position, if seriously pursued, can easily become a basis for perpetuating dictatorship. A constitution, which clearly defines the framework for the exercise of the powers of government, the rights and freedoms of the people as well as their political responsibilities, is an essential prerequisite for democratic government.

We further noted that some of those who appeared before the fora advocated a two-party system for Ghana. Attractive as this system may seem, *to decree a two-party system in Ghana would be a clear restriction on the freedom of association for it would seem that those whose social interests and political beliefs are not catered for by the two parties decreed would have no avenue for full political expression.* It should therefore be left to practice to determine the number of parties the country should have.

We have also observed attempts in the course of the discussions to set up the military against the civil population and *vice versa*. The MFJ finds this approach unhealthy and likely to create a siege mentality among our soldiers. Our soldiers are part of Ghanaian society and experience essentially the same joys, difficulties and struggles as other members of the society. There was also the challenging view that the "armed forces have become a *de facto* political constituency", and that any future political arrangement must recognize this reality if it is to avoid military intervention. This view flies in the face of the most elementary democratic principle of equality of citizens and tends to make a whole nation of 14 million people hostage to some 15,000 armed men. It is a viewpoint pregnant with many dangers for the democratic future of the country and must not be encouraged.

We believe however that no one can ignore the question of military intervention in any discussion of the future system of government for our country, not in the sense that the military, as an institution, must have a specially carved out place and role in the system of government, but in the sense that any future system of government must address the important question of military interventions. In the view of the MFJ, this is essentially a practical political problem — the conduct and practice of political parties and politicians, particularly those who hold office, their sense of dedication and service in the interest of the people and commitment to the principles and rules of multi-party democracy; the need for a new orientation and education of our force and service personnel on their role and responsibilities to society.

On the basis of the foregoing observations, the MFJ presents to the nation what it believes should be the subsequent phases in arriving at a democratic system of government for the country.

1. Either the PNDC recognizes the overwhelming demand for multi-party democracy and bows to the inevitable, or it has no alternative but to put the no-party system as against multi-party democracy to the test of a national referendum.
2. In the event of a national referendum, we consider a 6-month period of campaign prior to the referendum reasonable. In order to ensure that the campaign proceeds in a free and open political atmosphere, all repressive laws must be repealed. Both the multi-party and no-

party viewpoints should have equal access to the state media — national papers, radio and television. The Newspaper Licensing Law, in particular, must be repealed to enable all views to find free expression.

3. The referendum should be organized by an*i* *ndependent Electoral Commission*. The Commission should be composed of: 2 representatives of government; elected representatives of organized labour; representatives of farmers; an elected representative of the student movement; elected representatives of the religious bodies; elected representatives of the professional bodies; a representative from the National House of Chiefs; a representative from the security services; a representative of the MFJ; and representatives of other democratic organizations. Where the multi-party position is carried in the referendum, the ban on party political activity should be immediately lifted.
4. After the referendum or where the PNDC concedes to the popular demand for multi-party democracy, an *independent Constitutional Committee* should be established to prepare a *draft constitution* within 3 months. This committee should be made up of representation similar to that of the Electoral Commission.
5. Following the completion of the work of the Constitutional Committee, the Committee should present the draft constitution to a *Constituent Assembly elected on the basis of universal adult suffrage* for discussion, amendment, enrichment and promulgation.
6. Following the promulgation of the constitution for the Fourth Republic, free and fair national elections should be held.
7. The voters register should be re-opened for the referendum and the elections since many Ghanaians, for diverse reasons, did not register in 1967.

There should be no attempt by the government to stampede Ghanaians into a hurriedly organized referendum or national elections under government control to give it undue political advantage as has recently happened elsewhere on the continent.

The MFJ believes that these processes are necessary if we, as a people, are to achieve a system of government that enjoys the support and confidence of all Ghanaians. At the same time, the requisite political atmosphere for free expression must be created through the repeal of all repressive laws in the country. In making these proposals, we do so from the perspectives of contributing to a peaceful and open process of building democratic institutions and a democratic culture in our country. It is our hope that the PNDC government will respond to the genuine sentiments that inspire our proposals by addressing them in a spirit of dialogue and free *(sic)* of prejudice. We call on all Ghanaians to rally behind these proposals as an open and democratic process that will ensure that the people of Ghana themselves decide the system of government they want. Let us not lose this opportunity for a peaceful solution to the question of our future political system.

Signed:

Johnny F.S. Hansen
(1st Vice Chairman)

Obeng Manu
(National Secretary)

Dan Lartey
(National Treasurer)

Kwame Wiafe
(National Executive Member)

John Ndebugre
(National Organizer)

Ray Kakraba Quarshie
(2nd National Vice-Chairman)

Akoto Ampaw
(Executive Member)

Kwesi Pratt, Jnr.
(Deputy National Secretary)

A. Owusu Gyimah
(Executive Member)

B. K. Nketia
(National Executive Member)

DOCUMENT 4

Statement by the National Union of Ghana Students on the Political Future of Ghana — Issued on the 4 September, 1990

[ ] You are welcome to this morning's conference at which the NUGS' position on the political future of our dear nation, Ghana is to be made known through you to the entire populace and to the international community. This is not the first time we are stating our position on the political system of Ghana. What we wish to state now has been made *(sic)* several times in the past by way of congressional decisions or memoranda; perhaps the only difference is within the context of the current national debate which was initiated by the PNDC Chairman at Sunyani. Before stating the overwhelming consensus reached by our Central Committee on 3rd-4th August, 1990 at the Accra Polytechnic, it is very important to make known certain observations of the Central Committee, concerning the ongoing national debate.

It is very unfortunate that this Press Conference is being held when what is supposed to be a national debate seems to be more *(sic)* of a one-sided affair. Precisely, the district assemblies which are already limited in their exercise of duty par *(sic)* statute and functioning, happen to be the major conduit pipes as well as the platform for a process that is supposed to be for everybody. It is well registered that with the one-third *ex-officio* membership of the district assemblies and the political headship being an appointee of the PNDC, freedom of expression at the level of the district assemblies is circumscribed. The picture is being painted that multi-partyism and a system of government based on the district assemblies are two opposing political concepts for which the choosing of one necessarily means the rejection of the other, i.e. by the nature of official utterances and general reports on the debate. The inevitable impression is that whoever is for multi-party democracy is against the concept of decentralization and *vice versa*. This is not only misleading but fraudulent as well. Our affirmation is that decentralization, i.e. town, local and district council administration is necessary in the effective performance of any attempt therefore to put the issue as a system of government based on district assemblies versus multi-partyism will serve to play assemblymen against the rest of the public.

"History repeats itself", so it is widely known but the past of Acheampong's UNIGOV in the later 1970s apart from the impressive record of no execution for political offences, could also be referred to as a period within which a military regime appointed a fair, firm and impartial electoral commissioner in the person of Justice Abban. Perhaps it may be for the 'mistake' Acheampong made by appointing such an electoral commissioner that under Rawlings' National Commission for Democracy (NCD), Justice D.F. Annan, a member of the PNDC and Vice-Chairman for that matter has been made the NCD Chairman. Even the unborn knows the outcome of a case in which the presiding judge is the defendant. This situation lends itself the more to a *fait-accompli* programme especially when no time-table on the debate has been made public. Moreover, the manner of reaching and publicizing a national consensus is yet to be known. The most gullible will understand the intentions of the PNDC regime. Yet, to guard jealously the extremely powerful influence of the regime on the district assemblies, some PNDC functionaries have ostensibly welcome *(sic)* ideas from all political persuasions but do not stop at rationalizing to near-absolutism, a non-terminal point to the 31st December coup d'etat. The latest "running with the hare and hunting with the . . ." demagogy came from the Chairman of the PNDC himself and was published as a banner headline story in the People's *Daily Graphic* of Monday 27 August this year. According to the publication, Flt. Lt. J. J. Rawlings called on Ghanaians to participate fully in the on-going debate but stated that "the district assembly reflects the honest choice of the people and as such the people would not take any insult or incitement against the assembly". Does this imply that a position which is not in support of the district assemblies means an insult to the assembly or that the PNDC wants all Ghanaians to fall in line and to accept a no-party dictatorship? Practically, what confirms our primary observation is the blatant distortion as well as harassment of those who have so far openly declared their position in favour of pluralistic political alternatives. Needless to mention the intimidation of the executives of the Kwame Nkrumah Revolutionary Guards and the Movement for Freedom and Justice who have so far advocated for a multi-party system. Our determination however is to blaze a trail through this forest of harassment and intimidation so as to fulfil our unshirkable responsibilities.

One cannot deny that the media is the mirror of society and effective vehicle for dissemination and articulation of the views of the citizenry. However, it is highly irregular to observe the excessive regimentation and manipulation of the Ghanaian media so much that their reportage of dissenting views is near absurdity. Save some foreign media organizations, whose interest might not be the same as what our local media should have, the state-owned media have virtually become the publicity *gendarmes* for the government-managing suppressions and dealing firsthand attacks to those whose ideas do not conform to the status quo.

The most outrageous of the apparent "freeze" on the people's right to popular expression, balanced flow of information, and to a free debate is the PNDC Law 211 which apart from stifling the few independent and impartial press in contravention of article 19 of the Universal Declaration of Human Rights, gives the newspaper an extremely wild and wide definition. The Newspaper Licensing Law empowers the PNDC government to determine who is deemed fit to publish, what to publish, and under which conditions. The overall effect is the promotion of mediocre journalism aimed at diverting attention from contestable issues.

We wonder how well a national debate can be generated when the combined effect of PNDC Laws 91 (the Habeas Corpus Amendment Law) and 4 (Preventive Custody Law) makes it possible for the regime to order detention without trial for an unlimited period of anyone who in their judgement is suspected of endangering the security of the state. It is rather devious to think of a national debate when so many people are being held in detention by the PNDC for political reasons and many are in forced exile.

[ ] Who is free without daring to speak on such a madethorny *(sic)* political issue when some aspects of the PNDC Law 78 gives the PNDC government the legal right to execute Ghanaians for political offences — its definition and justification entirely at the discretion and prerogative of the PNDC.

With the formation of the Bureau of National Investigations and the Civil Defence Organization as well as the turning out of loyal uniformed men; notwithstanding the fact that most of its members have become revere *(sic)* sycophants and strikingly, lawless elements in the society, we are actually at a loss as to the safety of those who might perceive the political future of Ghana from a different perspective. Given the fear, suspicion and intimidation arising out of the aforesaid and their consequent influence on the political culture of Ghana, we wish to submit the following as an *interim sine-qua-non* for a healthy political development.

1. That all oppressive laws namely PNDC laws 4, 91, 211, 224 and other totalitarian laws be repealed to boost the morale of the citizenry to free expression, association, movement, worship, etc.
2. That all political prisoners be unconditionally released from preventive custody.
3. That a general amnesty be granted to all political refugees to

enable them participate in the politics of the country.
4. That a Press Commission with members drawn from identifiable groups be established to safeguard the freedom of the press.
5. That the Civil Defence Organization, the Bureau of National all Investigations (BNI) and the personal security corps be abolished to prevent the harassment and brutalization of innocent people and to save the nation from huge financial expenditure.
6. That the National Commission for Democracy (NCD) be dissolved and reconstituted with membership drawn from identifiable social and political groups in the country with a guaranteed autonomy from the PNDC.

Much as we endorse the idea of decentralization based on local or district council administration, we reject emphatically a new political arrangement founded on the present district assemblies because evidence abounds in the section of the PNDC Law 207 (Local Government Law) providing the legal basis and framework of the districts, that the PNDC wants to entrench itself in power. Section 11, subsection 2, paragraph (g) of the PNDC Law 207 specifies among the functions of the Executive Committee, to work to strengthen the National Democratic Revolution. Though the district assemblies partly comprise elected representatives, the PNDC has the power to dissolve any district assembly at will. This certainly jeopardizes the existence of any assembly that refuses to dance to the tune of PNDC's voice at any point in time. It is interesting to know that though the District Secretary is a member of the assembly and the Chairman of the District Executive Committee, his office is higher than the Assembly.

Apparently, the regime has an irreversible forethought. To marginalize pluralism with the simple reason that the multi-party system engenders corruption, strife, division and nepotism is to downplay the point that military administrations apart from the physical and psychological violence they unleash do actually thrive on those political evils. It is our conviction that a constitutionally elected civilian government under a multi-party arrangement is capable of accommodating all the differing opinions within the glaring multi-sectoral context of the Ghanaian citizenry. At least, under a civilian constitutional arrangement of this nature, certain unpopular policies such as Junior Secondary School (JSS), present Educational Reforms, Structural Adjustment Programme (SAP), etc. cannot be advanced with impunity as now.

Moreover, freedom of the press under a constitutional arrangement could, to a reasonable extent, be guaranteed since the recognition of opposition is a necessary condition for the objective performance of the press.

[ ] Multi-party democracy has not been given the chance to thrive in Ghana by populist military take-overs. What we are therefore calling for NOW is an atmosphere in which dictatorship would be seen not only with the contempt it deserves but as a blatant violation of fundamental human rights and a direct affront to the rule of law, peace and progress. At this juncture, we recommend that:

1. The National Debate should not be restricted to a four-cornered room in each region, but should be extended to market places, institutions, et cetera to enable the entire populace to share ideas together.
2. Following the debate, a free and fair referendum should be the means of determining the national consensus on the political future of Ghana. The referendum must be organized by a body whose sympathies would not be narrow but all-embracing.
3. Whatever discussions on our political future should culminate in the formation of a Constituent Assembly which would draft a Constitution for the return to multi-party system of government. Political parties should be funded by the state.
4. Membership should cut across ethnic, religious, and sex groupings. Any trace of TRIBALISM should be a basis for disqualification.

We implore all Ghanaians to be fearless, defiant, and resolute in the quest for democracy based on the proper consent and approval of the people.

Note must be taken of what Emperor Haile Selaasie I of blessed memory said sometime ago and which is quoted, "THROUGHOUT HISTORY IT HAS BEEN THE INACTION OF THOSE WHO SHOULD HAVE ACTED, THE INDIFFERENCE OF THOSE WHO SHOULD HAVE KNOWN BETTER AND THE SILENCE OF THE VOICE OF JUSTICE WHEN IT MATTERED MOST THAT HAS ALLOWED EVIL TO TRIUMPH."

Issued on Behalf of the Central Committee of the National Executive Committee.

Daniel Owusu-Nyampong
(National President)

Paul Asare Ansah
(Co-ordinating Secretay)

Michael Obeng
(National Treasurer)

Akwasi Afriyie Asante
(Editor-in-Chief)

DOCUMENT 5

Resolutions of Ghana Bar Association at its Annual Conference in Accra, 30 September to 4 October, 1990

A. Whereas the people of Ghana are presently engaged in the establishment of a Constitutional, democratic structure for their governance

Whereas the Ghana Bar Association has consistently called upon the PNDC Government to restore the country to democratic civilian rule based on multi-party politics

Whereas to this end the General Council of the Bar has submitted to the 1990 Annual Conference of the Bar a memorandum on the principles that should animate the future Constitution of the country, which has been adopted in its entirety

Whereas the Ghana Bar Association believes that the operation of a democratic system is the best way of ensuring accountability in our national life

Whereas the PNDC Government has recently notified the African Charter on Human and People's rights

NOW THEREFORE THE GHANA BAR ASSOCIATION resolves as follows that:

1. The conditions must be created now for a return to a Constitutional civilian democratic order in Ghana and that to this end,
2. All constraints on the freedom of expression should be removed forthwith. Therefore licensing and censorship of the press should cease and the government's rigid monopoly of the mass media should cease.
3. Freedom of assembly must be permitted so that the public may freely hear views and opinions other than those of the government and the current discussion about a future constitutional order may be fuller and the people may more readily form and express their opinions.
4. All detention without trial and all political detention must cease and any person detained on political grounds must be released forthwith. Those detained on suspicion of having committed a crime must be quickly tried.
5. A Constituent Assembly must be set up which should complete

its work within six (6) months and should be elected on the basis of universal adult suffrage in single member constituencies country-wide. It should be clothed with the power to promulgate a new Constitution.
6. Pending the setting up of a Constituent Assembly a Constitutional Committee should be appointed forthwith to examine the previous Constitutions of independent Ghana and suggest any modifications it may consider necessary in the light of experience and submit its recommendations to the Constituent Assembly.
7. The National Commission for Democracy which in its present form is an integral part of the PNDC should be abolished. Finally, the Government should appoint an independent Electoral Commissioner to put into place the mechanism for the setting up and the election of the Constituent Assembly and future elections.

B. Whereas the functioning of an impartial and independent Judiciary is fundamental to the effective Rule of Law,

Whereas the Ghana Bar Association has taken note of the fact that current Laws give the PNDC Government power to remove judges of both the superior and inferior Courts at will,

Whereas in furtherance of the Rule of Law, it is essential that security of tenure of Judges be properly assured and guaranteed.

NOW THEREFORE the Ghana Bar Association resolves as follows:

PNDC Law 145, which gives the PNDC power to remove Judges at will, should forthwith be repealed and that removal of Judges should be effected only on grounds of infirmity, mental or physical, or for stated misconduct pursuant to a procedure which gives a fair hearing to the Judge or Judges concerned. Further, appointment of Judges should be made in accordance with the advice of the Judicial Council, and not on the current basis of recommendations by the Judicial Council.

C. Whereas it is essential for the safeguarding of the Rule of Law that justifiable disputes between citizens of this country be resolved by normal judicial processes,

Whereas the practice has grown whereby such disputes are being dealt with by extra-judicial bodies, to wit the revolutionary organs such as the CDRs, CDOs, and Militia,

Whereas the unchecked growth of such practices will fatally undermine the Rule of Law in this country,

NOW THEREFORE the Ghana Bar Association resolves as follows:

The PNDC Government should take immediate steps to ensure that such practices are brought to an end.

D. Whereas the members of the Ghana Bar Association are mindful of the fact that there are some lapses in the administration of justice existing from unnecessary delays in the trial of cases, from the paucity of the necessary modern equipment for the efficient functioning of the Courts, from the pitiful salaries of the members of the Judicial Service, and in some cases from the unethical conduct of members of the Bar and Bench,

Whereas the Ghana Bar Association is anxious to address these concerns with a view to improving the administration of justice in the country.

NOW THEREFORE the Ghana Bar Association resolves as follows:

The General Council of the Bar should make regular representations to the Chief Justice and the Attorney-General to address these problems, and also the General Council should take steps to revive the practice of regular meetings between the Bar, Bench, the Faculty and the School of Law in order to achieve the end of an improvement of the administration of justice.

E. Whereas the Ghana Bar Association is particularly mindful of the difficult economic circumstances confronting the country, particularly as a result of the recent, dramatic increase in the prices of petroleum products,

NOW THEREFORE the Ghana Bar Association resolves as follows that:

The PNDC Government take steps to ensure the proper management of the country's economy so that a decent standard of living can be assured the people of this country.

F. Whereas the Ghana Bar Association wishes to congratulate the the Namibian people on their accession to nationhood on the basis of a democratic system of government, elected on the principle of universal adult suffrage,

Whereas Ghana Bar Association is glad to note that the prospects for the establishment of democracy in South Africa has been greatly enhanced by recent events, most notably the release of Nelson Mandela and other political prisoners, and the unbanning of the African National Congress and other political movements in South' Africa,

Whereas the Ghana Bar Association is concerned about the recent factional strife amongst the black population of South Africa,

Whereas the current situation in Liberia gives cause for great concern to all citizens of West Africa,

Whereas the invasion of Kuwait by Iraq poses a grave threat to world peace and stability.

NOW THEREFORE the Ghana Bar Association resolves as follows that:

1. It expresses its solidarity and complete sympathy with the black people of Azania (South Africa) in their struggle for freedom and independence in accordance with the United Nations Charter and the Universal Declaration of Human Rights and that in order to accelerate the pace of this struggle it calls upon the black people of Azania to bury all their differences and close their ranks and fight as one people with a common goal and destiny.
2. All the warring factions in our sister Republic of Liberia should endeavour to lay down their arms, respect a ceasefire and contribute to the establishment of peace in Liberia and the construction of a government on the principle of one-man-one-vote.
3. The Ghana Bar Association condemns the invasion of *(sic)* Iraq of Kuwait and calls upon it to withdraw unconditionally from Kuwait in accordance with various UN resolutions on the issue.

Dated at Accra this 4th day of October, 1990.

(Signed) Nutifafa Kuenyehia
(National Secretary)

DOCUMENT 6

A Memorandum to the Government of the Provisional National Defence Council from the Christian Council of Ghana on "Ghana's Search for a New Democratic System of Government"

[PREAMBLE]
As servants of GOD ALMIGHTY entrusted with the Leadership of the Church of JESUS CHRIST in this country, and called, also to be co-partners with GOD in the continuing creation we, the Christian Council of Ghana, the Heads of whose Member Churches have appended their signatures below are, accordingly, dedicated to GOD'S TRUTH AND JUSTICE. We cannot but be concerned with the socio-political, economic and other issues which affect our country.

As a free association of some of the major Christian Churches whose membership is spread throughout Ghana, the Christian Council has always taken a non-partisan position on political issues. Nevertheless, we deem it our duty to encourage our Membership to express their political opinions freely and responsibly, and to ensure that those views and convictions are heard and duly respected.

It is for these reasons that we give thanks to the ALMIGHTY GOD for the opportunity He affords us to examine our political situation in Ghana again. We furthermore appreciate the atmosphere created by the Government of the Provisional National Defence Council (PNDC) which has stimulated the search for a new democratic form of government for our country, and to which the Christian Community has appropriately responded.

The Christian Council is aware that the Church in Ghana has a prophetic role to play, in witnessing to the truth in all matters affecting the welfare of our people, and a sacred responsibility to create a suitable climate for reconciliation and, thereby promote understanding and forgiveness. It is in this way that bitter revenge may be avoided, and a calm and peaceful return to a Constitutional Democracy ensured, for the spiritual and moral well-being, and the material prosperity, of the Sovereign People of Ghana.

In accordance with its objective of enabling its member Churches, and their several Congregations, to express their political beliefs and aspirations freely and responsibly, the Christian Council in October and November, 1990, initiated a FORUM for discussion throughout its constituencies, and a SEMINAR also, as machinery for the examination of that national question, and collation of those opinions and sentiments on the new quest for democracy.

This MEMORANDUM therefore represents the CONSENSUS emerging from the processes set in motion. We accordingly state that consensus as follows. We implore the PNDC Government to acknowledge and respect these opinions as the voice, and will, of our people, and ensure urgent action on these recommendations:

Steps Towards Restoration of Civilian Rule

1. We urge that after staying in power for almost ten (10) years now, the Government of the Provisional National Defence Council should take immediate steps to return the country to Civilian Rule under an administration fully mandated by, and accountable to, the people of Ghana, not later than December, 1992.
2. In that regard, therefore, the PNDC Government must LIFT THE BAN ON PARTY POLITICAL ACTIVITY, by the end of January, 1991, as an essential and assuring step towards the attainment of that Constitutional Democratic Administration.
3. To that end, we recommend that the appropriate LEGISLATION be immediately promulgated setting the scene, and the right atmosphere, for the FORMATION OF POLITICAL PARTIES of the people's own free choice. Each one of those Political Parties should be truly national in character, broad-based and also cut across religious, and ethnic lines.
4. We urge, also, that political prisoners under detention, and all those being held under various forms of political restraints, be immediately and unconditionally released and discharged. And that a GENERAL AMNESTY be immediately declared in favour of Ghanaian refugees and exiles abroad.
5. We wish to stress that, in the interest of peace, harmony, stability and goodwill in the country, all legislation that suppress, inhibit and curtail the people's human rights: freedoms of speech, expression, association, worship, etc. must be abrogated.
6. We urge that a CONSTITUENT ASSEMBLY composed of Representatives of such identifiable groups as formed part of previous Constituent Assemblies, supplemented by other bodies which have, subsequently, emerged be established, by the end of March, 1990:

(a) to write a NEW CONSTITUTION for the Nation, using our Constitutions of 1969 and 1979, together with any other relevant ones, as working papers;

(b) to continue to incorporate the principles of the 1948 United Nations Declaration of Human Rights in the Constitution.

7. As a pre-requisite for preparations toward the formation of Political Parties, and the setting up of the Constituent Assembly, we advise that an independent and autonomous Electoral Commission be re-established:

(a) Such a re-establishment shall also serve to demonstrate the PNDC's good intentions of returning the country to Democratic Civilian Rule.

(b) The State shall allocate to the re-established Electoral Commission, adequate funds and logistic support, to facilitate the discharge of its electoral functions.

(c) It is expected that adequate legislative and administrative precautions will be taken to eliminate electoral frauds and mal-practices, in aid of free, honest, and fair elections and referenda.

(d) To this end, we urge that our electoral processes shall be held throughout the country simultaneously on one fixed and certain date; fragmented, or scattered, elections encourage electoral frauds, and mal-practices.

(e) All our elections should be SECRET, and through the BALLOT BOX by universal adult suffrage.

Constitutional Proposals

8. The consensus was that the 1969 and 1979 Constitutions were widely acceptable and should be adopted as the basic constitutional documents for review.

9. The independence of the Press must be guaranteed in the Constitution. To achieve this, we also recommend that the country's PRESS AND MEDIA BE PRIVATIZED, to operate independently of Government's involvement and control. The Government shall, therefore, neither own, nor run any Newspaper in the country. Where the Government desires to inform, or to advertize to the general public, it shall do so through its own Gazette, Press Releases and Conferences, and Periodic Bulletins. On the other hand, Political Parties may own Newspapers, Magazines, etc. It is recognized that the Radio and Television at this stage in Ghana's development cannot be privatized and therefore should be organized under independent Corporations, and substantially funded by the State.

10. We further advocate that an independent PRESS COMMISSION be established, under the country's Constitution, to oversee the affairs and concerns of the Press and other mass media, Newspaper Licensing laws, etc.
11. We urge that the JUDICIARY of this country be competent, free and independent, to be able to safeguard the honour and esteem of justice, liberty, and of law. This independence must be guaranteed in the Constitution.
12. We acknowledge that our Traditional Chiefs should carry around them an aura of honour and statesmanship. This should put them above partisan politics, to preserve the reverence due to their exalted office:
    (a) It is the consensus, furthermore, that our Traditional Rulers continue to serve the nation through the various Houses of Chiefs. They may also be appointed either to the Council of State, or to such other organs of State as shall not compromise the awe and reverence due them.
    (b) We advise that the Government exercises no right of involvement in the selection of destoolment of our Chiefs. To guarantee the integrity and independence of our Chiefs, serious consideration should be given to restoring some traditional independent sources of funding the stools and skins. Government funding of Chiefs should be restricted to expenses incurred in attending public meetings and functions on behalf of the nation.
13. We urge that the independence of the Church and other religious bodies be guaranteed in the Constitution to ensure the freedom of worship envisaged in the United Nations Declaration on Human Rights.
14. We acknowledge that the DISTRICT ASSEMBLIES have come to stay as essential elements in the administration of the State:
    (a) We nevertheless urge that membership to them should be through universal adult suffrage and mainly on party political lines and that they should have a life-span of four (4) years, and be restructured to exclude from their membership, Government-nominated candidates.
    (b) The District Assemblies should also *not* be Electoral Colleges for Parliament.
    (c) No District Assemblyman should be a member, simultaneously, of both the District Assembly, and of the National Parliament.
    (d) The office of the District Secretary should be elective, and his functions determined by the Constitution.

15. We acknowledge that as citizens of Ghana, our Military, Police, and Civil Servants ought not to be excluded from exercising their political rights. But where they seek political office, we urge that they must first resign their office and position.
16. We advise that an OMBUDSMAN be appointed under the Constitution, of the status of a Justice of the Superior Court of Judicature. He should have Regional offices under his administration, with the requisite independence, and facilities, to be effective in the discharge of his functions.
17. We advise that an independent Organization be established, to enlighten the people on democracy, government, and their rights and responsibilities, and true patriotism. The need has never more been urgent, than now, for the emergence of true leaders who fear God and respect the rights and sensibilities of the people of Ghana. For this reason, we submit that respect for law, and commitment to discipline, good order, and justice in the country must be promoted at all levels of our Ghanaian society, because these are conducive to peace, stability and harmony. This must be seen as being consistent with the Christian's witness in the promotion of the Kingdom of God and His Righteousness on earth.

Conclusion

18. We pray, therefore, that the HOLY SPIRIT of the LIVING GOD who has graciously sustained and preserved this country, may lead all of us in the paths of truth, humility, brotherliness and understanding, to work hard with tolerance and fearless honesty, towards a just, peaceful and prosperous country. It is our earnest prayer also, that this Nation shall then be filled with the Glory of God, even as the waters cover the sea.

Respectfully submitted.
Signed by Heads of Member Churches:

Name of Church

1. Rt. Rev. D.A. Koranteng, Presbyterian Church
2. Rt. Rev. F.W.B. Thompson, Anglican Church
3. Rt. Rev. K.A. Dickson, Methodist Church
4. Rev. (Maj.) W.A.K. Agbenya, E.P. Church
5. Rev. S.T. Okrah, Mennonite Church
6. Mr. David Acquah, Society of Friends

7. Rev. Francis W. Sey, A.M.E. Church
8. Rt. Rev. Paul K. Fynn, Lutheran Church
9. Col. M. Y. Obiri, Salvation Army
10. Rev. Kojo Osei-Wusuh, Baptist Convention
11. Rev. Dr. G.N. Zormelo, A.M.E. Zion Church
12. Bro. Yeboah Koree, Feden Church (not available to sign)
13. Rev. J. Yenn-Batah, C.M.E. Church
14. Rev. Fr. K. J. A. Labi, Orthodox Church.

Affiliated Organization
15. Mr. A. A. Sarkodee, YMCA
16. Mrs. Kate Parkes, YWCA

Rev. David A. Dartey
(General Secretary)
CHRISTIAN COUNCIL OF GHANA
December 17, 1990.

DOCUMENT 7

The Catholic Church and Ghana's Search for a New Democratic System

Introduction

The Catholic Church has watched with known interest the recent debates on the future of the country. She considers the fact that the debates took place and continue in some, though muted, form as a welcome development, in spite of all the imperfections. This development can augur well for the future of this country. The Church is further encouraged by some aspects of the New Year broadcast to the nation by the Head of State.

In the past, the Church has on occasion expressed herself on various aspects of the nation's welfare. Now that a national debate has been sparked off by the government itself, the Church feels an even greater responsibility to make herself heard. She considers this as a continuation of her spiritual mandate. She hopes that her contribution will encourage others to join in this quest for principles and structures for the future governance of this country.

At the outset of this contribution, the Church wishes to make it clear that, in her view, the future survival of this country depends on the fashioning of structures and the development of principles and ideas which will nurture constitutional rule. This requires a careful admixture of management with belief and efficiency with conviction. In the view of the Church, any approach which extols one of these values to the exclusion of the other can only spell disaster in the long term.

Government is a tool for the advancement of the interests of the people of a society. Therefore any system of government for the future must be designed to promote, firstly, the well-being of the people and, secondly, a congenial environment for socio-economic development.

In the following we, the hierarchy of the Church, intend to direct attention to some of the key issues that must be examined in this new search. Especially, we want to lead our people to recognize the importance of human rights, traditional Ghanaian values and stable institutions that could guarantee freedom, justice and individual as well as national progress.

HUMAN RIGHTS

We are firmly convinced and strongly advocate that the pursuit, promotion and protection of fundamental human rights must be made an important element of any future constitutional arrangements for Ghana. Human rights enable us to live our lives in decency, security and with dignity. Their pursuit enables us to fulfil vital needs such as food, clothing, shelter, health care and education in a healthy atmosphere. This is why in recent times human rights issues have received so much increased attention from the international community. The Church firmly believes that the neglect of human rights at the domestic level can have only disastrous consequences and possibly threaten world peace. The evidence seems incontrovertible that countries which plunge the world repeatedly into war begin by thought control of their citizens.

In stressing that our constitutional arrangement for the future governance of this country should provide adequately for the due observance of human rights, we should not be seen as merely articulating and pandering to another yoke of our colonial experience. Human rights provide a vital linkage between traditional values and modern needs of good government. For we have to remember that long before post-war international institutions became concerned with human right issues, various social and political systems existed in Africa and definitely in the communities that make up modern Ghana, which gave legal recognition to the rights of people, their privileges and responsibilities. Our pre-colonial societies were concerned with social inequalities, anti-social conduct, greed and the issues of free speech. Our folklore is rich and replete with evidence of the manner in which they were articulated and the strategies devised to deal with rulers who persistently violated them. Indeed, the Church believes that the time has come for our future constitution to go one step beyond Chapter 6 of the 1979 Constitution by establishing a special human rights court to deal solely with human rights disputes.

The human rights landscape has changed worldwide. There is greater awareness that it is futile to struggle for wider socio-economic reforms without human rights, and this explains why international solidarity for human rights has increased. The United Nations Universal Declaration of Human Rights is now accepted embodying universal values of decency which must be recognized by every constitutional system and integrated into it. Here in Africa, our governments recently elaborated an African Charter of Human and Peoples Rights. The Charter represents progress of great significance to the development of and respect for human rights on our continent. It provides, among others, for non-discrimination, equality, the right to information, freedom for religious worship, the integrity of the family and respect for community as well as individual interests.

But by far the most important contribution of the African Charter, in our opinion, is the fact that it does away with the false divide between civil and political rights on the one hand and the social, economic and cultural rights on the other. We have noted in the past our happiness that our government has ratified this Charter. We now propose that its provisions be integrated into our future constitution to enable the people to enjoy the benefits which its ratification should bring to them.

TRADITIONAL HERITAGE AND MODERN DEMOCRACY

The search for a system of government that takes cognizance of Ghanaian traditional cultures is without doubt an imperative and a historic task. Out traditional cultures contain modalities of public behaviour and proper conduct of affairs of state which deserve to be carefully studied and incorporated into our structures for modern government.

Indeed the people of Ghana have, since the era of colonialism, been governed by a dual mandate: the mandate of traditional rule which is defined by the authority structures and norms of the traditional constitutions and the mandate of the modern state, which transcends all the ethnic groups and unifies them into a new polity. One major issue for any contemporary constitution-making process is how to harmonize the two mandates through structures that would assist Ghana to evolve as one nation and enjoy good government, peace and progress.

In respect of norms, our system of traditional leadership has a lot to teach us. The following are some of the ideas inherent in many forms of traditional leadership roles. They express universal values that need to be secured in any future constitutional set-up.

1. *The Ideology of Service*: In many parts of Ghana the chief swears to serve his or her people, and they in turn swear to serve him or her.
2. *The Oath*. The Oath spells out to the chief the norms by which he or she should rule, and underscores the fact that power and authority derive from the people alone.
3. *The Rule of Law*: The chief is subject, by the oath of his or her office, to the law of the land.
4. A chief does not exercise personal power. He or she submits his or her opinion and judgement to the collective wisdom of the people as expressed by the council and private advisers who regularly consult the people and speak for them.
5. While consensus is the mode of deciding on collective issues, it calls for the need to solicit and listen to all shades of opinion. It was

pro verbially asserted that one head did not go into council; and no heads were excluded because it was held that the word of wisdom might lie in the head of the fool.

6. Our traditions respect human rights, and the obligation to protect life was jealously guarded by the state. Thus, in some places, inexplicable suicide was regarded as an offence that required the corpse of the suicide to be brought to court. The chief before whom the corpse was brought judged and 'executed' the corpse for presuming to take his or her own life. The right of speech was affirmed as a means of securing life and was expressed by the saying "he who did not permit me to speak is an evil person". Similarly, the right of association was expressed in various proverbs as a necessity of life.

7. Finally, traditional culture saw power as stable only when shared. Paradoxically egg-like, "power should not be held too loosely — it would drop; or too tenaciously — it would be crushed". Power was not to be held in one hand; by its nature it has to be shared. This is Ghanaian traditional wisdom.

These are ideas and values whose relevance to modern government cannot be over-emphasized. They reflect universal ethical values enshrined in many democratic constitutions. The effort to identify these universal values with indigenous principles and traditions can serve two important purposes: first, to counter those who often point to these principles as alien to Ghana; and second to enhance popular understanding and acceptance of them through appropriate idiom.

It is worth remarking how those who drafted our previous constitutions endeavoured to reflect in them the most important of these values and structures. Specific mention may be made of the following:

1. The Ombudsman: Traditionally our societies have had groups of identifiable people with their head whom aggrieved citizens could approach to protect their rights (see Chapter 11 of the 1979 Constitution).
2. The Council — or the Elders — to advise the President and create a forum where partisanship gives way to impartial discussions and consensus is achieved to facilitate parliamentary decision-making. (See Chapter 10 of the 1979 Constitution.)
3. The recognition of chiefs and the various Houses of Chiefs as an integral part of the modern governmental apparatus. (See Chapter 19 of the 1979 Constitution.)
4. The seating of Chiefs in Local Councils and Development Committees. (See Article 56 of the 1979 Constitution.)
5. The power granted to citizens to impeach the President and get him deposed. (See Article 56 of the 1979 Constitution.)

6. The protection of the freedom of assembly and association as well as the recognition of freedom of speech as an inviolable human and civil right. (See Articles 28 and 29 of the 1979 Constitution.)

The time has come for us also to look at, and exploit to its fullest potential, some structures created in recent times for channelling the expertise, experience and influence of traditional leaders into the processes of modern government, namely, the Regional Houses of Chiefs and the National House of Chiefs. Some may argue that these institutions are not indigenous to the traditional constitutions. Yet there is no doubt that these institutions give a national dimension to the deliberations of our traditional leadership. Together with the representation given our chiefs on local government structures, they serve to ensure that the chiefs do not see themselves as parochial dignitaries or potentates. After the experience of thirty-four years of independence, the case for thrusting these institutions deeper into the mainstream of our modern central governing machinery hardly needs to be argued.

Representative Government and Popular Participation

Since the earliest attempts to mould our various peoples into a single nation began, there have been two major constitutional concerns for the populations, namely, representative government and popular participation. True representation requires a credible electoral process. Elections, because they deal with choice, naturally engender conflicts. It is important therefore that we address issues of election and conflict in our present search for democracy.

At the outset, it must be stated that conflict need not be disruptive or destructive. Indeed true democracy has no place for destructive conflict. If the traditional symbol of the Siamese crocodiles tells us anything, it is simply that while peoples and groups seek their collective good, they may yet fight. This is why there was no traditional African political system, homogeneous or heterogeneous, that did not recognize the reality of conflict in society and especially in politics.

It is not without significance to the current debate to note that many of our traditional societies have formal groupings which were sociopolitical units particularly prone to confrontation and conflicts. In all contests for chiefly office upon a vacancy, we see evidence of interest, sometimes organized groups, born out of competition for political office. Thus, while the elections to the district assemblies make it quite attractive to examine the merits of elections without group or party politics, it has to be appreciated that a small local community where votes can be canvassed on personal basis cannot be likened to a national constituency.

In spite of what in a different context we ourselves have said in the past, we have come to the considered conclusion that group or party politics is essential to the factors which service the processes of true democracy and political pluralism.

Political parties perform two very basic important and unavoidable functions in a constitutional democracy. Firstly they give expression to an important bulwark of constitutionalism for the people, namely, their freedom to join forces with like-minded fellow citizens in pursuit of their legitimate objectives. Secondly, they provide the nation with group of individuals with a perception that goes beyond localized interests and which is translated into national programmes or plans ready for implementation after election. That being the case, in our view, political realism and the national interest should lead us towards a multi-party system in which rules can be openly formulated to regulate its manner of operation. In this connection, we believe that all that is necessary is the reintroduction of Article 42 of the 1979 Constitution.

In coming to this position, we would like to draw attention to the disturbing fact that even though we are living in a state in which there are supposed to be no parties there are a host of movements and organizations, committees, etc. which in all but name carry out the functions normally performed by political parties. We have no reason to believe that such groups will dissolve themselves or be liquidated in the future.

They thus enjoy undue visibility, advantage and power. A continuation of this situation in which the neutrality of such groups cannot be taken for granted, and is in fact contradicted by their activities is clearly unsatisfactory. We believe that all individuals and groups are entitled to a fair chance of organizing and mobilizing public opinion and this can be done only within the framework of political parties for the reasons we have already given above. It is in the light of this development that we now consider that the inevitability of party politics in any modern society should be recognized and appropriate structures established to ensure its smooth operation. This makes it imperative that the ban on political activities be lifted as soon as possible so that fairness and equity may be guaranteed for all. The present situation appears to be giving a heard-start to certain groupings.

STRUCTURES OF REPRESENTATION

District Assemblies

In pursuance of a new political system for our country, the PNDC government introduced the concept of the District Assemblies.-The establishment of District Assemblies in which at least two-thirds of the members are directly elected and which are regarded as the highest political authorities in the districts is a good idea. In enacting the District Assemblies Law, whose main aim is to decentralize power to the district, the PNDC Government has taken a positive step to provide for grassroots participation in government and put the power of self-development in the hands of the people.

However, laudable as the concept is, there is every indication that all is not well with the Assemblies, for several reasons. The Assemblies are of different social and economic circumstances, and it seems as if for some districts they do not exist at all. In some areas, poor infrastructure has hindered the work and overtaxed the dedication of even the most enthusiastic members.

Then there is the question of the relationship between the legally created Assemblies and the several other organs which are also prominent in the districts. This is creating the problem of authority conflicts, as District Secretaries, Assemblymen and women, CDRs (Committees for the Defence of the Revolution), TDCs (Town Development Committees) and traditional rulers appear to vie for power and limelight in their communities. It would be most helpful if the government could decline (sic) each group's area of authority and jurisdiction.

In view of the topic of the recent fora, one would have expected the Assemblies to offer a critique of the Law establishing them and to relate their experiences and difficulties after its two-year operation with a view to reform and improvement. But the contributions of the Assemblies appear to have been, with a few exceptions, an exercise in self-praise. Some regarded the Assemblies as stepping stones to higher levels of power and even proposed that the term of office of the Assemblymen and women be extended from three to five years. The three years stipulated by the Law are enough in our estimation.

Regional Assemblies

The next step in the quest for a suitable political system should be the establishment of Regional Assemblies which will focus on the problems of regions as opposed to those of districts. These Assemblies will co-ordinate the activities of the various districts as well as liaise between the districts and government. They will hopefully ensure the equitable distribution of the resources of a given region among the various districts.

During the seminars organized by the National Commission for Democracy, certain misgivings were expressed about Regional Councils by some of the speakers, but not all the reasons offered were convincing.

One hopes that these misgivings were not the result of the fear that the Regional Councils and the Regional Councillors will overshadow the District Councils and the District Assemblymen and women. It must be stressed that the needs of a given region may not be identical with those of a given district and that a person chosen at the district level may not be the best person to represent the region when it comes to the regional or national level, since the issues involved are much larger and more complex, and require a higher level of expertise and experience.

One problem that may arise in connection with the Regional Assemblies is the danger of regionalism, or regional patriotism that may be carried too far to the detriment of national unity. In the future political system, some constitutional safeguards will have to be found to prevent this from happening.

National Assembly

In addition to the Regional Assemblies, we would want a National Assembly elected for four or five years by universal adult suffrage. This will be in line with Article 76 of the 1979 Constitution. This Assembly or National Parliament will address issues of national importance.

Finally we would want to see the Head of State of Ghana elected by the same process with a term of office of four or five years renewable only once. This will be in accord with Article 50 of the 1979 Constitution which talks about the election of the President.

THE OPEN SOCIETY

The Mass Media

As we have said time and again in the past, the mass media play a vital role in any society that aspires towards democracy. It is through the media that information is disseminated, different views are shared, ideas are confronted, public opinion is formed and consensus achieved. In addition to providing avenues to the government to obtain feedback on its performance, it also acts as a safety valve by enabling citizens to express their views. So vital is the role of the mass media that freedom of expression, and, by extension, of the press has been called "the first freedom". Any successful assault on fundamental human rights almost invariably starts with a suppression of the freedom of the press. Once this freedom is denied, the authorities can play havoc with the other fundamental human rights without any publicity.

Freedom of the press is possible when there is a diversity of sources of information, so that issues can be considered from different angles.

It is for this reason that we propose that in our future constitution, as in the 1969 and 1979 Constitutions, freedom of expression and of the press should be guaranteed. We think that there should be no law requiring individuals or groups to obtain a license for the establishment of a newspaper, journal or other channels of communication. But even before we get to the stage of promulgating a new constitution, we strongly urge that in order to create an atmosphere conducive to a free and frank exchange of ideas, the Newspaper Licensing Law (PNDCL 211) should be repealed immediately to enable citizens to choose the medium through which they can make their contribution to the on-going debate.

An objective assessment of the performance of the press in this country clearly shows that the periods during which there was a relative measure of freedom of expression and of the press were under the Second and Third Republics. The Third Republican Constitution had, in its Chapter 22, provisions on the Press Commission. Though the Press Commission was not a perfect institution in its composition or operation, it was the nearest that we have ever got to providing ourselves with the vehicles for the public expression in this country. It is no wonder that after the coup d'etat of December 1981, the Ghana Journalists' Association and some other groups expressed the view that even though the Constitution had been abrogated or suspended, that particular section of the Constitution should be allowed to operate. The journalists certainly must have known what they were talking about. We therefore strongly urge that the Press Commission idea should be looked at carefully with a view to reintroducing it, purged of all the weaknesses detected in the original arrangement.

On the same issue of press ownership and control, the view has been expressed in certain quarters that the daily newspapers should be privatized and removed from government control. It is recognized that the government of the day needs channels for making its programme, priorities, plans and achievements known to the public to mobilize support for development. But it is a fact that the government has a whole array of facilities at its disposal including the Ministry of Information and the Information Services Department for the performance of such tasks. Experience has shown that where journalists see themselves as the direct employees of government, they become inhibited in the performance of their professional duties.

However, we would also like to caution that a privately-owned press system does not by itself guarantee press freedom. The interests pursued by owners may not always coincide with the public interest. What all this means in effect is that this issue must be made an important part of the agenda for public discussion so that in the light of our experiences and needs in this country, we fashion a press system that will help promote development while giving the people ample opportunity to express their views on national issues. Diversity of sources of information is an essential ingredient of the freedom of expression and we pray that we shall live in an environment that politically, socially, culturally and economically favours the nurturing of a free and independent mass media system in which the varied views can find legitimate expression.

Independence of the Judiciary

The growth of democracy can be measured by the freedoms that citizens enjoy, especially by their right of access to the institutions that safeguard and enhance the security of their rights and freedoms. Thus access to law to seek one's rights and protect one's interests is vital to the life of a democratic society, and this can be guaranteed only by an independent judiciary.

It is evident that an independent judiciary is indispensable to constitutional democracy. Therefore we would advise that, as was the case with the 1969 and 1979 constitutional instruments, the principle of the neutrality of the process of judicial appointments and loss of office, the inviolability of the conditions of service and the security of tenure of the judges must all be adequately provided for in the constitution. Further, all necessary legal strategies must be employed to insulate the judiciary against partisan politics.

We are not unaware of the fact that the independence of the judiciary ultimately proceeds from the judges' resolve, their fidelity to their judicial path and their adherence to principle. Candour, however, compels us to admit that principled professional conduct requires in our context the conscious creation of a legal environment in which it can flourish. Especially in our African countries, judicial independence depends also to a large extent on the willingness of the executive to accept the mandate and mission of the judiciary.

From our recent experience, we have noticed another factor which undermines the independence of the judiciary, and indeed ultimately the administration of justice as a whole. This is the fragmentation of judicial power as presently exists between the regular courts and the public tribunals. We accordingly propose that before any new constitutional arrangements take effect, the public tribunals should be brought under the regular courts.

OTHER ISSUES

Measures of Stability

The instability of government in many African states is caused by military takeovers. We need to find solutions to this problem. To this end we note that no measure of stability can be guaranteed where the basic needs of a people are not satisfied. Care must however be taken not to make the pursuit of food, shelter and clothing the only yardstick for deciding on the kind of constitution we should have. It is human beings that produce these things, not constitutions.

In our considered opinion, the following may be crucial in any discussion of how to ensure political stability in Ghana:
1. Good government;
2. Respect for the constitution by all sections of the nation, namely, the government as well as the civilians but particularly the military;
3. Equitable distribution of the nation's wealth;
4. The inculcation of the courage to protest against a bad governent by peaceful means;
5. Commitment to collective vigilance;
6. General discipline of the army and civilians;
7. General training in non-violent resistance against unconstitutional tional takeovers.

Of all the factors enumerated above that can affect political stability in the country, the non-violent resistance factor appears to be the most decisive, because even a good government can be overthrown for one reason or another.

It is important to bear constantly in mind that out of 33 years of our independence, civilian governments have ruled for a total of 14 years with the last two Republics sharing between them less than five years. The remaining 19 years have been shared by military governments. Our efforts at building democratic traditions have therefore often been frustrated and interrupted by coups d'etat. These interventions have annihilated the opportunities available to us as a nation to mature politically.

It is also important to remember that military intervention in politics does not come about as a result of a representative, collective decision taken by the Armed Forces as an institution. It would rather appear to be the result of an action undertaken by a tiny group of officers and/or men fired by some ambition and idealism. The rest of the Armed Forces fall in line once power has been seized, but the initial act of seizing power is hardly collective. It is very important to underscore this fact of the unrepresentativeness of military regimes even among the military, in view of the claims to representativeness often made by coup leaders.

The reason why a small group of soldiers takes over a whole country is that there is a monopoly of power held by the Armed Forces. Once they know that there is the possibility of resistance from the rest of the population, they will not too easily attempt to seize power. Hence our suggestion above concerning education in passive or non-violent resistance in order to protect the integrity of the nation.

The Church and the Secular State

We believe that the members of the Church as citizens of the nation, have the same political rights and obligations as the other citizens. The political responsibilities of Churches can find support in the saying of Jesus, "Render to Caesar the things that are Caesar's, and to God the things that are God's (Mk. 12:17). Thus we urge all our members to take an active part in the current debate and to make their views heard on the political future of Ghana. If they fail to make their views known, others will decide their political destiny for them. Whether as assemblymen and women, or members of identifiable groups or even as members of future political parties, they have to be actively involved in the political life of the nation.

However, we also reaffirm our belief that the Church as an institution cannot and should not indulge in partisan politics. The Church cannot identify itself with any political party or with any regime, since this would compromise her objectivity and impartiality and make it difficult for her to speak out prophetically in denunciation of injustices that may be perpetrated by the regime with which she is identified. The Church should, however, always seek to cooperate with the ruling government in the attempt to improve the quality of life of the people.

The Regional Seminars and the Role of the NCD

The recent seminars on the political future of Ghana organized by the National Commission for Democracy (NCD) need to be evaluated critically in the interests of our dear nation. The idea of a public debate on such an important issue is indeed laudable. Some of our countrymen and women have used the opportunity provided to express themselves genuinely. However, the manner in which the seminars were conducted compels us to make a few comments.

First of all, one can question the "public" nature of these seminars which, by and large, were limited to the Assemblymen and women. Even though a few other people got the opportunity to speak at these seminars, it cannot really be claimed that those who spoke were drawn from the different strata of our Ghanaian society, given the disproportionate time that was allowed the Assemblymen and women. Secondly, it is debatable to what extent the discussions were "free", in view of the continuous presence of government officials on the very platform where the participants spoke which could be intimidating. Thirdly, the requirement that all those who wanted to participate in this national debate could do so *only* under the umbrella of the National Commission for Democracy threatened the freedom of expression and of the right peaceably to assemble and petition the government; it was also irreconcilable with the principle of participatory democracy expressed by the PNDC Government.

In this regard, we hope that other groups or movements wishing to hold their own discussions on the political future of this country will be allowed to do so and not be treated like the Movement for Freedom and Justice (MFJ) in their bid to inaugurate a branch in Kumasi or to organize a symposium at the Bediako Hall in Accra.

Time-Table for Return to Constitutional Rule

Even though public debates have been organized by the National Commission for Democracy in the regions about a return to constitutional rule, there is as yet no clear indication of any time-table spelling out the various stages of the expected evolution. In the recent New Year speech of the Chairman of the PNDC we have been given a partial view of a programme, but nothing has been said about the ultimate stages. This is clearly unsatisfactory, and the earlier an unambiguous time-table was set, the better it would be for the country.

We believe that the political education initiated by government-sponsored organs has gone on long enough, and it is time the ban on political activities was lifted to enable citizens to form their own groups and choose their own platforms to take part in the process of educating the public about their rights and duties as citizens.

In connection with the time-table for a return to constitutional rule, we would also suggest that public officers, both civilian and military, who would like to take part in the elections as candidates should resign their public offices at least nine months before the elections or forfeit their right to present themselves as candidates. This is to ensure that such people do not use the various platforms that their public offices give them to undertake campaigning at the expense of those who are not in a similar position.

From what one has been hearing so far from official statements, it looks as if the government-appointed NCD will be charged with the function of handling elections, as it did for the District Assembly elections. If this is true, it might cause some uneasiness among some people. To allay any fears, we propose that an independent body should be set up to handle purely electoral matters from registration to actual polling; in other words, the NCD should be divested of its electoral functions and a proper Electoral Commissioner's Office established.

On the voting process itself, it is our considered view that the system which was used in the 1969 and 1979 elections as well as in the "Union Government" referendum should be adhered to, in order to minimize the opportunity for rigging and other abuses. However, we believe that to further reduce the possibility of abuse and corruption of the electoral process, a fool-proof method for identifying the voters should be devised. In this regard, we take note of the statement made by the Chairman of the PNDC in his New Year address to the nation that national identity cards will be issued in the course of the year to all citizens.

On the specific details of a time-table, we propose a return to full constitutional rule by the end of 1992. A Constitutional Review Committee can be empanelled to review the 1979 Constitution in the light of any new ideas which have come up since then. The Committee should be able to complete its work within a specified period. The final draft which emanates can later be submitted to a referendum. Elections can then take place throughout the country at a date to be fixed, after which the newly elected government would assume office.

We propose that as much as possible everything should be done to make the transition to constitutional rule a deliberate process. For this reason we urge that the government should create a climate which makes for genuine and effective participation by all our people in the constitution making process. Those who have constructive ideas as well as those perceived from government perspective, as having negative views only, are all entitled to be heard. In this connection, we request the repeal of the following decrees which we consider to be against some of our basic human rights: (a) The Preventive Custody Law (PNDCL 4); (b) The Habeas Corpus (Amendment) Law (PNDCL 91); (c) The Newspaper Licensing Law (PNDCL 211); (d) The Religious Bodies Registration Law (PNDCL 221).

In asking for a return to representative, constitutional rule, we are not unaware that at the district level there is some representation of the people in the governance of the districts. Neither are we asking that the Assemblies be dismantled. We are merely asserting the widespread feeling throughout the country that the Assemblies cannot be taken as a substitute for a truly national representative government empowered by the people through free and fair elections to take important policy decisions affecting the destiny of our country.

Conclusion

Having delivered ourselves of the opinions expressed in the preceding paragraphs, we do recognize that we have not been able to cover all the topics and relevant issues. We do believe, however, that we have covered enough grounds that constitute a contribution to the on-going national debate on the return to constitutional normalcy in our country. We are also realistic and humble enough to recognize that not everybody will agree with the views we have expressed or even the manner of putting them across; this is normally to be expected in a sophisticated society such as ours with a tradition of independent thinking. However, we consider that in contributing to the national debate, we are only discharging our responsibility both as citizens and as spiritual leaders because as we have pointed out earlier, Christians have a duty to participate fully in all aspects of national life. We are also convinced that it is out of a free exchange and confrontation of ideas that there will emerge some consensus on how we shall govern ourselves in the years ahead.

If there is one issue out of the several we have raised that we would like to draw special attention to in this conclusion, it is that of the timetable for return to a truly national representative government. We believe that in sound management practice the relation of objectives to target dates enhances proper planning. We therefore consider that the vagueness surrounding a fixed date for return to constitutional normalcy is undesirable and advise that this issue be addressed candidly by the PNDC without any further delay.

We also consider it necessary to draw the attention of our compatriots to the fact that whatever constitution that finally emerges from the discussions will not be perfect. This calls for preparedness of the nation to amend and adapt our institutions in the light of our experiences and changing circumstances. This is the only way in which we can build a tradition of orderly evolution of institutions. To achieve this, we need patience, tolerance and a spirit of give and take, so that we can evolve in an orderly way and build solid foundations of constitutionalism.

Finally, in association with those other groups that have made a public call for a return to a genuinely representative, constitutional democratic rule, we must emphasize that we are only articulating and claiming what is properly due us, namely our right as citizens of an independent state whose motto is "Freedom and Justice" to have and to enjoy a meaningful participation in the manner in which we are governed.

20th February 1991
(Sgd.) Rt. Rev. Peter K. Sarpong
Bishop of Kumasi
PRESIDENT, CATHOLIC BISHOPS' CONFERENCE OF GHANA
for and on behalf of
CATHOLIC BISHOPS' CONFERENCE OF GHANA

Section Two
1991

Introduction

Clearly by the close of 1990 the military government was under considerable pressure to open up the politics of the country to allow democratic participation in the pursuit and exercise of power, in the choice of who governs the country, and respect human rights. By then events in Eastern Europe and in South Africa had added further weight and urgency to the legitimacy of the demands of the pro-democracy forces. The donor community was also insisting on democratic political reforms by all the authoritarian regimes which were running terribly weak economies — like Ghana's PNDC — as a condition for receiving additional aid.

In spite of the weight of these internal and external pressures the PNDC government remained unruffled and adamant. Indeed it was under pressure but not demoralized. It had not even lost enough domestic legitimacy to compel it to bow, however slightly, to the hurricane of democratic demands. The reason was simple: it still enjoyed the support of core functionaries of the Committee for the Defence of the Revolution (CDR). These remnants of the PNDC's revolutionary past saw their future tied irrevocably to the survival of the regime itself by a combination of material (pecuniary) and political considerations, which were purely private and dictated primarily by their survival instincts. The PNDC government enjoyed support also from the new crop of grassroots (sub-regional) elites who had been brought into the political limelight by that government's decentralization policies. It should be recalled that the district assemblies had been intended as the super-structure of a future national representative institution that would emerge from the PNDC's programme of grassroots democracy. The grassroots elites, numbering about 6,589 and scattered throughout the 110 district and metropolitan assemblies of the country therefore regarded themselves as a strategically placed hegemonic bloc with a stake in the PNDC's agenda for grassroots democratic politics. For them too the stake was both pecuniary and political. There were also other so-called revolutionary and quasi or para-military organs — like the Mobisquads, Civil Defence Organizations, others like the Ghana Road Transporters Union of the GTUC, a number of associations representing informal sector operators and, above all, the leadership and functionaries of the 31st December Women's Movement.

The rank and file of these associations and elite groups were an enormous political resource for the PNDC. They constituted a formidable counter-force to the swelling pro-democracy forces, and successfully mobilized grassroots support for the government especially during those challenging moments. With their support the PNDC government could remain firmly in control of the content of the transition programme as well as the direction of the transition politics in general. The confident political posture displayed behind the 1991 new year's day broadcast to the nation by the Head of State, J.J. Rawlings, which outlined a transition programme was derived from such immense political support. Yet that speech left the pro-democracy forces in no doubt. The reactions to it and to subsequent events in the transition programme reflect the irrepressible determination of the pro-democracy forces to oppose the PNDC government's intransigence and unresponsiveness to their demands.

DOCUMENT 8

Broadcast to the Nation by the Chairman of the PNDC, Flight-Lieutenant Jerry John Rawlings on Tuesday, 1 January 1991

[ ] Once again a year has come to a close and I would like to take this opportunity to wish you all peace and happiness in the new year and pray that God will continue to bless and guide us in the years ahead...
[ ] The message of the 31st December Revolution was not just about a change in the economic circumstances of the nation. It was also about giving power to the people and ensuring their full participation in the processes by which they are governed. It was also about making democracy a daily reality in the lives of our people.

It was in this spirit that four years ago, on the 5th Anniversary of the Revolution, I announced a new momentum in our march towards an effective and stable democratic order. It provided for district assemblies which were to become the pillars upon which the people's power would be erected. The District Assemblies were to become the focal points of development at the village and town levels. The principle of popular participation was given meaning through the assemblies, where decisions directly affecting the lives of the people were to be taken.

The objective of the elections was for a system of local government of the people, by the people and for the people. In other words, it was for a system that gave the voters power to exercise control over their own affairs.

For once, we witnessed clean and healthy elections which resulted in the genuine political expression of our people. Having established the authority of the people and having created the solid foundations for participatory democracy throughout the country, it does not make sense for anyone to want to disregard the Assemblies and create other institutions or structures that have no integral or organic relationship with the district political authorities. It is therefore very disappointing to say the least, to hear statements from people who are expected to know better, seeking to marginalize the authority of the people that is finding expression in the district assemblies.

Indeed when the idea of elections to the District Assemblies came up, a number of people with the same outlook, saw in it, an outcome that would oppose the revolutionary process. But by turning out in their numbers to vote for their true representatives, the people rejected the pretensions of those yesterday's men and their new-found allies.

If history has any meaning for us it could only be right that we sought a better way to build secure foundations at the base of our political and administrative structures. That was our agenda and I made it clear then, that once we had given ourselves time for the foundations to solidify, we would take further steps towards erecting the national structures.

The assemblies which were inaugurated almost two years ago have since demonstrated a tremendous capacity to serve both as the vehicle for development and a truly representative voice of the people.

The respectable men and women in the Assemblies have continued to grow in experience and competence bringing a measure of self-confidence, initiative and community pride to Ghanaians, who under previous governments had been assigned the role of passive on-lookers in the affairs of government.

It is the policy of the PNDC to continue to encourage and assist the people of this country to exercise in every possible way, their legitimate rights as citizens of this country.

Government is, however, aware of the numerous problems facing the Assemblies and is equally concerned that they do not just exist but are viable enough to carry out the developmental and other very important functions assigned to them.

To this end, the financial provisions of the Local Government Law have been reviewed and two additional sources of revenue namely the daily transport tax and advertisement tax have been ceded to the assemblies. It is expected that these two sources alone will make available to the assemblies, over one billion cedis in 1991.

The distribution of the revenue accruing from the two taxes will be done bearing in mind the financial circumstances of the various districts. It is not beneficial for one district to have resources to build roads for instance when other roads leading to that district are impassable. Revenue sharing will therefore, as far as possible, be on the basis of the principle of equal and balanced development. In addition to these and other measures, steps will be taken to ensure the full implementation of the programme for the decentralized departments.

Government is aware of the tendency on the part of some departments to undermine the authority of the district assemblies, claiming to report only to their head offices. There have been cases where requests by the districts for vital information have been turned down because the personnel of the departments concerned still refuse to understand the new order in local government administration.

This year the full authority of the assemblies, within the limits of the Local Government Law, will be brought to bear on the operations of the decentralized departments in the districts. The punitive transfers of some dedicated assembly members outside their electoral districts will be stopped and those already carried out will be investigated . . .

[ ] As we begin our march towards the tenth milestone, it is important to re-state the political objectives of the 31st December Revolution in order to correctly project our thoughts into the future of the political process. It is also important to remember some facts about the on-going process.

We began this process of democratization and restructuring long before there was any sign of the changes that we have witnessed in Eastern Europe; long before anyone heard of Glasnost or Perestroika and the opportunistic demands being made in certain quarters today in the name of democracy. We began on our own because we deemed it right, because we were faithfully and fundamentally dedicated to the realization of true democracy in our land, and because we faithfully and sincerely believed that the only way to free the latent energies and talents of our people and have them channelled into positive pursuits was to them the right to control their own affairs in a democratic manner.

But you know as I do, that this is not the first time we have been talking about building a democratic society. It was on the agenda during our struggle for independence and it has been on the agenda ever since. We have tried many constitutions and each time faltered along the way.

The democratic ideals that we yearn for require the commitment of all of us, and we will only be committed if we understand the implications of these ideals for all aspects of our lives.

Government is not the only body required to practise democracy between itself and members of the public but it is a fundamental requirement amongst human beings. We cannot profess the ideals of democracy and yet deny its practice in our homes, our work places, in our unions and in the churches or armed services to which we belong.

Democracy is not just about forming political parties and contesting elections. Indeed we have seen the paradox of political parties whose mode of internal organization has been far from democratic and who have therefore themselves destabilized the very constitutional order they were supposed to be upholding even before any military coup took place.

It has to be the case therefore, that if we are seeking something that would endure, then we should not confine ourselves to the conventional theories of democracy to which we have become attached; and that we should rather stretch our imagination, tax our ingenuity, critically examine our past and recent experiences in the hope that we might fashion democratic structures that would be in accordance with our temperament and conditions as black African Ghanaians with our unique way of doing things as a result of who we are, where we come from and where we are going with our limited resources but abundant pride and intense desire to feel the freedom of our sovereignty.

That was why in July this year the National Commission for Democracy, began sounding national opinion on what the people saw as the way forward. From the contributions made at the various regional fora, it became clear that the trauma of repeated failures of previous constitutional models has generated fresh thinking among our people. [ ] I have my views and I would like to express them candidly. With our past experiences as a guide, I have had some reservations about a total reliance on some of the simplistic and superficial proposals that have been canvassed in the form of slogans and cliches.

I am also concerned about the undue emphasis being placed on the electoral process *per se* to the neglect of other important issues of democracy such as the role and rights of trade unions, the position of the security forces in the political machinery, equality of women, the rule of law irrespective of who you are, of the conditions or environment within which we in Africa conduct political campaigns and the electoral process and above all how to forge unity among our peoples. I sincerely believe that a serious consideration of some of these issues will enrich our discussion.

The NCD has held public deliberations at all the regional capitals where large numbers of Ghanaians freely articulated their views. I am aware the Commission is still receiving memoranda from all sections of the people and where possible, making themselves available for a dialogue with those who seriously want to contribute to the search for a rational and stable future for our country.

During the seminars organized by the NCD at the regional capitals, hundreds of individuals were heard as spokesmen and women for groups with similar interests, whether chiefs, lawyers, teachers, farmers, unionized labour, assembly members, women's groups and so on. In effect, the opinions of thousands of people were expressed, and these in turn were heard, whether on television, radio or through the press, by millions. Those in turn discussed what they heard at home, at work, in buses, in bars and under trees in their compounds all over the country.

[ ] I do not believe that it is necessary for the NCD to repeat the same formula of organized fora and debates at the District and lower levels. This is because despite the great success of the regional fora, there is a danger of the discussion becoming repetitive, diffuse and probably vague, or of becoming over-simplified and polarized, if we continue to go round discussing the same issues endlessly.

Our Assembly members, citizens, cadres, members of identifiable groups and well-meaning people in the districts will understand that when a man is chewing a piece of meat, it is perhaps best to swallow it before all the taste is gone.

Therefore, in order not to kill interest and enthusiasm in the process that has been initiated towards consolidating the democratic future, the NCD has been requested to present its report by the end of March, this year to enable the PNDC convene a broad-based national consultative body which would use the report as well as the 1957, 1960, 1969 and 1979 constitutions and other constitutions, as the basis for further consultations and discussions on the content and form of the future constitution. A group of constitutional experts will also be assembled to assist in setting the constitutional proposals into an appropriate legal framework. We expect that by this time next year, we would have completed steps that will give us a draft constitution. The NCD has also been requested to open the voters register in accordance with the electoral regulations by the end of the year and take the necessary steps towards the programme of issuing identity cards to all citizens of Ghana.

[ ] Our eyes are now dimly set on the final phase of our journey as a provisional government and on the road towards establishing for Ghana, a new constitutional order. But I believe we have learned, over the years, that a Constitution as a mere legal document is of no real value, however fine the language and however lofty the sentiments, unless it is a true reflection and embodiment of the perceptions and noble aspirations of ordinary Ghanaians. When a constitution embodies principles which are a consensus of the firmly held view and practical experiences of people from Axim to Bawku, from Hamile to Aflao, then no force can breach such a constitution, because it resides not in a piece of paper, but written with the blood of the people. In other words, the character of the constitution we envisage cannot be the work of any small group of people. Its contents must, as we have always been insisting, derive from our historical experiences and also from the democratic process set in motion on 4 June 1979 and 31st December, 1981.

It is my hope that each and every person who may be called upon during the coming year to contribute to this process of fashioning a living constitution, will do so with humility, clarity and a deep sense of responsibility towards the future of our dear Ghana.

[ ] It is time to take these steps into the future. It is not a blind leap, and it is not a question of merely following current fashions. We will proceed according to our Ghanaian pace not upon the dictates of those who peddle models and abstract prescriptions without paying attention to specific circumstances.

As part of the steps towards the preparation of the constitution, the Ghana Law Reform Commission will be tasked with the review of existing laws, with a view to harmonizing these to accord with the spirit of the provisions on fundamental human rights, as may be enshrined in the future constitution. The review is in line with the government's policy of ensuring that law reform is a continuous process that is in keeping with changes in social values and national aspirations.

Our concrete commitment to the pursuit of the fundamental human rights of the people, however, cannot be the same as those who merely find it fashionable to shout cliches and slogans on human rights and resort to rhetoric only to score debating points. Human rights cannot be limited to paper guarantees only, hence the various policies initiated by the government to promote the cause of human rights by improving the economic conditions that ensure the welfare of the average Ghanaian.

The government also recognizes the role of the press in the evolving democratic process and will accordingly take steps to constitute a national body on the media that will amongst others, ensure that the press both private and public, is adequately prepared for the higher responsibilities it must shoulder as we advance towards a new constitution. It is also envisaged that the body will foster the achievement and maintenance of the highest professional standards in the mass media. It is hoped that this new body would check those who hide behind the freedom of the press to publish misleading reports, and also protect the interests and security of journalists as well as the general public.

In addition to these actions, the PNDC will carry out a general re-organization of a number of organs including the Public Tribunals and the National Investigations Committee . . . [ ] The time has come for us to show mutual trust and tolerance. We may not all share the same ideas but we share the same destiny. We may not be particularly fond of each other but we need to be particularly tolerant of each other.

[ ] We stand at a crucial stage in our nation's history conscious of the destiny that beckons to us all. We must hold out a hand of reconciliation, of trust and confidence. The hand must be open to all who seek the future well-being of our nation.

I am not asking of anyone to abandon his interests nor am I asking for anyone to suppress his opinions. I am simply and deeply convinced of the need for harmony and co-operation, of a common vision, common objectives and above all for the unity of our nation. Let us embrace the spirit of the times we live in whilst realizing the spiritual values of our noble heritage.

And finally, may I wish you all again the goodwill of the season, and God's blessings in this New Year. [ ]

DOCUMENT 9

Statement of the Ghana Bar Association Made at an Emergency General Meeting of the Bar on 23 February, 1991 on the Programme for a Return to Constitutional Rule

In his New Year address to the nation, the Chairman of the Provisional National Defence Council, Flt-Lt. J. J. Rawlings, made pronouncements about his Government's intentions concerning the future governance of our nation which are of crucial significance to every citizen of our country. The PNDC Chairman indicated *inter-alia* that:

i) his provisional government was in the final phase of its existence, and to this end
ii) the PNDC had instructed the National Commission for Democracy, NCD, to submit its report on the deliberations of the recently concluded NCD-sponsored fora by the end of March 1991.
iii) consequent upon the receipt of the NCD report, "a broad-based national consultative committee" will be established to consider the NCD report, the post-independence Constitutions of Ghana, and any other constitution in order to draft by the end of 1991 a new, appropriate Constitution for the country.
iv) a group of constitutional experts will be formed to assist in this process of drafting a new Constitution.
v) the Law Reform Commission will undertake a review of the existing laws of the country with a view of harmonizing these laws with the dictates of fundamental human rights which will be embodied in the future Constitution.

The Ghana Bar Association warmly welcomes the commitment of the PNDC, to a restoration of constitutional rule for this country. This commitment represents in the eyes of the Association a vindication of the principled stance taken over the past few years by the Ghana Bar Association and other independent bodies such as the Christian Council of Ghana, the Trades Union Congress, and the National Union of Ghana Students on this vital matter of the need for a constitution for our country, a stance which in the past has drawn ill-considered and irresponsible criticisms from some quarters. Further it is the view of the Association, since there is now a general consensus on the need to restore the country to constitutional government, that the process of transition to a constitutional order set out by the PNDC Chairman be critically examined to ensure that the transition is effected peacefully, responsibly and in a manner that transparently satisfies the aspirations of the broad masses of our people. This statement represents the Ghana Bar Association's contribution to this process.

A critical examination of the PNDC Chairman's statement reveals certain crucial omissions in the programme as currently defined for the restoration of constitutional rule. It is the view of the Ghana Bar Association that it is essential that those omissions be rapidly remedied if the goal of peaceful transition is to be met, a goal which reflects the wishes of all well-meaning Ghanaians. The most glaring omission relates to the absence of a clear time-table for the return to constitutional government. Even though the New Year statement made reference to a draft constitution coming into being "by this time next year", it left out any reference to the elections which must be held under the new Constitution. We believe that this is a crucial omission which must be rapidly redressed. The essence of democratic government is the right of the people to choose their rulers by a free demonstration of their will expressed through a secret vote at the ballot box on the basis of universal adult suffrage. The Ghana Bar Association therefore calls upon the PNDC Government to give flesh to its intentions as expressed in the New Year statement by defining for the country a clear time-table for the return to constitutional government which culminates in the holding of free and fair national elections.

Another important omission in the New Year statement relates to the absence of any criteria for the selection of the "broad-based national consultative committee" which will be established to deliberate on the future constitution. The Association takes it that this "committee" is in substance a Constituent Assembly; for a rose by any other name is still a rose. In 1968 and 1978, the selection of the Constituent Assemblies was by identifiable groups. The Ghana Bar Association believes that the formulae used on those occasions are well-suited to the present task, and calls upon the government to give a clear indication to the country as to the basis of selection of the members of the Constituent Assembly. The work of the Constituent Assembly will enjoy the confidence and allegiance of the people only if the composition of the Assembly is chosen in an open, transparent manner which reflects the aspirations of the broad masses of our people.. A Constituent Assembly dominated by representatives of the so-called revolutionary organs and other nominees of the

PNDC will undermine that confidence and allegiance, a result that will surely bode ill for the future, orderly development of our country.

The third omission from the current programme is the absence of any reference to the manner in which the new Constitution will be promulgated. The Ghana Bar Association is of the firm view, having regard to our recent history, that the promulgation of the Constitution should be a matter for the representatives of the people gathered in the Constituent Assembly. This will obviate any possible future criticism of the Constitution being the partisan work of the current government, and will give the Constitution the democratic character and support it needs to command the allegiance of the people. The Ghana Bar Association therefore calls upon the PNDC Government to state openly that the new Constitution will be promulgated by the Constituent Assembly.

A fourth crucial omission is the absence of any reference to the vital necessity of reconstituting the electoral body that will supervise the process for the return to constitutional government. It is manifestly clear from the deliberations of the recently concluded fora that the NCD is an integral arm of the present government. It cannot therefore pretend to be an impartial arbiter of the democratic wishes of our people. It is thus essential that immediate steps be taken to establish a truly independent electoral body which will operate freely outside of executive control and interference if the constitutional process is to be conducted in an impartial and objective manner. The Ghana Bar Association therefore calls upon the PNDC, as a prerequisite for a meaningful process of restoration of constitutional rule, to disband forthwith the NCD and to replace it with an independent Electoral Commission with responsibility for demarcating electoral districts and for supervising the conduct of the various elections that will result in the restoration of constitutional government to this country.

The Ghana Bar Association notes with approval the decision of the PNDC to institute a process of review of our existing laws for the purpose of bringing them into conformity with the requirements of fundamental human rights that the new Constitution will embody. Thus all those current laws which permit the detention of a Ghanaian citizen without trial, which restrict the freedom of expression of a Ghanaian citizen, which interfere with a Ghanaian citizen's freedom of religious belief, and which hamper the freedom of assembly and association of a Ghanaian citizen will have to be repealed if the democratic future which the majority of our people seek is to be realized. The Ghana Bar Association believes that this process of repeal must be initiated immediately if the deliberations on our future Constitution are to be conducted in an atmosphere devoid of fear and insecurity. A constitutional debate conducted against a background of repressive laws and measures will not be a debate worthy of its name. The Ghana Bar Association therefore calls upon the PNDC to demonstrate its sincerity to the goal of making an acceptable Constitution by repealing forthwith PNDC Laws 4, 78, 91, 211, and 221 which bear upon the liberty and freedom of expression of citizens of this country. The Association is in this regard particularly pleased to note that the process of law review will embrace the operations of the NIC and the Public Tribunals, hopefully with a view if not to their outright abolition but at least to bringing their operations within accepted norms of lawful conduct.

The Ghana Bar Association is of the view that the most effective guarantee for this process of restoration of constitutional rule is the enactment by the PNDC of legislation that will clearly set out the timetable and steps involved. Such an enactment will bear concrete, open testimony to the declared intention of the PNDC Chairman that his government is now in the final stage of its provisional life, and reassure the Ghanaian people that the dawn of a new constitutional era is indeed within sight.

The Ghana Bar Association would like to conclude this statement by making a solemn appeal to both the PNDC and the people of this country. We have yet again a historic opportunity as a people, to fashion for ourselves a democratic system of government, which will embody the universally accepted principles of democratic government — freedom of speech, freedom of association, freedom of assembly, freedom from arbitrary arrest, and freedom of religious belief. We can only effectively grasp this opportunity if our search for the democratic order is devoid of intolerance and rancour, vituperation and personal abuse. We can only progress as a people if our national affairs are conducted on the basis of humility, patience and a mutual respect for each other's views. Then the vision of the founding fathers of our state that the development of Ghana be founded on the twin principles of freedom and justice will at long last be realized.

DOCUMENT 10

Statement by the Movement for Freedom and Justice (MFJ) on the New Year Broadcast of the PNDC Chairman and Other Related Matters at a Press Conference in Accra, 11 January 1991

[ ] The National Executive Committee of the Movement for Freedom and Justice (MFJ) has found it necessary to invite you to this press conference because of the highly significant political events that marked the close of 1990. The two major speeches by the Chairman of the PNDC on 31 December, 1990, to our soldiers at the El Wak stadium and on 1 January , 1991, portray what can only be regarded as fundamental policy positions of the PNDC on the programme towards the future system of government for the country and the character of what the regime envisages should be that system.

These important speeches must therefore be studied critically by all Ghanaians so as to assess the extent to which the views expressed in them are in agreement with the democratic aspirations and interests of the people of this country. Above all, these policy positions should be assessed in relation to the viewpoints expressed by the independent and representative organizations of the people.

While there appears to be some shift in the position of the PNDC in the New Year broadcast, there are nonetheless other factors that suggest that the government may have other intentions. The speech at El-Wak, the general vagueness and ambiguity of the New Year broadcast itself, as well as the subsequent threatening editorial in the "Ghanaian Times' of January 3, 1991, to the effect that those who refuse to accept the "irreversible logic" of the December 31st "revolutionary process would crash into self-destruction at the dead-end" suggest that the PNDC may not have abandoned its stand for a no-party system as against the freedom of association and multi-party democracy.

We note that all the major independent political, mass and professional organizations in the country, as well as the churches, have called for multi-party democracy based on fundamental human rights in the most explicit terms. It is therefore most regrettable that the PNDC Chairman's speech on New Year's day did not make any direct comment on this demand. The omission cannot be regarded as a mere oversight.

This view is reinforced by the statement in the same speech that "Democracy is not about forming parties and contesting elections". The references to "our own unique way of doing things as black African Ghanaians", thereby suggesting that multi-party democracy is foreign to the "African way", and the negative remarks about "conventional theories of democracy to which we have become so much attached" and about "slogans and cliches" also confirm the above interpretation of the New Year Speech. In our specific Ghanaian situation of today where there are too diametrically-opposed viewpoints on the political future of the country, one for multi-party democracy, and the other for a no-party system, such comments can only be interpreted as a thinly-diagnosed position against multi-party democracy.

[ ] Among the elements of an apparent shift in the position of the government, we note that for the first time, the PNDC has admitted that human rights are imperative for any democratic system of government, though this admission appears, in the same breath, to have been undermined immediately by the observation that "our commitment to the pursuit of fundamental human rights of the people cannot be the same as those who barely find it fashionable to shout cliches and slogans on human rights". There has also been a recognition that a constitutional order is necessary and that all the past civilian constitutions of Ghana *which enshrined the rights of the people to associate freely in political parties* should be used as a guide in the drafting of the new constitution for the Fourth Republic. The speech also recognized that the struggle to build a democratic society has been on the agenda during the anti-colonial struggle and ever since, and not a profound programme of the PNDC. The PNDC Chairman further admits that there are laws in the country that are likely to be in conflict with the fundamental human rights of the people. He also admits that a constitution cannot be the work of a small group of people and that the rule of law is important in any democracy. In addition, the PNDC Chairman has called for "mutual trust and tolerance" and "reconciliation". The question however is whether these apparent shifts touch the heart of the issue of political democracy.

The continued resistance by the PNDC to democratic freedoms and principles is clearly manifested by the fact the PNDC Chairman failed in his New Year speech to respond to the very specific democratic demands that have been made by all the major independent political and mass organizations. In the first place, the speech says absolutely nothing about the hundreds of political prisoners and detainees who continue to languish in the prisons and the repeated demands for their release. There is equally no response to the demand for unconditional amnesty for political exiles. Above all, the regime continues to maintain disturbing silence over the specific demands for the repeal of particular decrees that are clearly repressive, namely: the Preventive Custody Decree (PNDCL 4), the Habeas Corpus (Amendment) Decree (PNDCL 91); the decree on newspaper licensing (PNDCL 211); the decree on the registration of religious bodies (PNDCL 221); and sections of PNDCL 78 dealing with execution for political offences. All these have been and continue to be the key demands of democratic forces in the country which are necessary to create an atmosphere conducive to free and open debate and to the personal security of Ghanaians to enable the people of this country decide in freedom the system of government they want.

The statement that "the Law Reform Commission will be tasked with the review of existing laws with a view to harmonizing these to accord with the spirit of the provisions on fundamental human rights, as may be enshrined in the future constitution" is no response to the concrete demand being made. It would be simpler, and promote mutual trust, if the PNDC went ahead and repealed those repressive laws forthwith. Furthermore, according to the time-frame of the PNDC, the Law Reform Commission can only do its work after the draft constitution has been produced. In contrast, the demand of the people is that these repressive laws be repealed immediately. In the spirit of "establishing a culture of respect for the most insignificant seeming member of our society", as the PNDC Chairman put it, the PNDC should show respect for all the major independent organizations of our land by acceding to their demands, which after all are in accord with building democratic institutions and a culture of democracy in the country.

The PNDC Chairman's New Year speech also evades other fundamental demands made by the people. There has been complete silence over the demand for a national Constitutional Committee made up of representatives of specific independent public organizations, and government representation, to draw up a draft constitution which would then be placed before a Constituent Assembly, elected on the basis of universal adult suffrage for discussion, amendment and promulgation. This demand contrasts sharply with the PNDC's policy in the New Year speech to set up an undefined "broad-based national consultative body" whose functions are extremely vague, namely to "use the NCD report as well as the 1957, 1960, 1969, 1979 and other constitutions as *a basis for further consultations and discussions on the content and form of the future constitution*". This particular policy leaves the whole nation in the dark as to what body will draw up the constitutional proposals, and which, according to the New Year speech, "a group of constitutional experts" (assembled presumably by the PNDC) will "assist 'in setting . . . into an appropriate legal framework". There is also no indication as to which body will promulgate the constitution. The MFJ has no doubt that the involved wording, vagueness and ambiguity of this crucial aspect of the New Year speech is certainly not a result of any difficulty in clear and precise expression, but of a deliberate policy of confusing the people. *Ghanaians must therefore demand, and the MFJ is accordingly demanding that the PNDC clarifies, in the simplest terms possible, what it is actually proposing to the nation.*

The proclamation that the PNDC will "take steps to constitute a national body on the media" is equally hazy as regards the composition of the body. It is also unclear what degree of independence from government control the body will have. It is thus not an adequate response to the specific and simple demand for an independent press commission made up of representatives of independent public organizations, such as the GJA, TUC, NUGS, GNAT, ARPB, etc. and of representation from government. Furthermore, a major obstacle to the development of a critical and objective press has been the obnoxious Newspaper Licensing Decree, PNDCL 211, the repeal of which has been demanded by the people. The refusal of the regime to repeal this unpopular decree takes added significance when it is recalled that the New Year speech appears to be more concerned that the proposed body on the mass media "check(s) those who hide behind the freedom of the press to publish misleading reports" than with the real problem of government control of, and interference with, the state media, and the lack of independent press media.

Another important demand of the people has been the call for the replacement of the PNDC's NCD by an independent Electoral Commission. This demand is based on the legitimate ground that the NCD cannot play the neutral role expected of it given the character of its composition, especially the role of its chairman, who is also a member of the PNDC. The instruction to the NCD to present its report on the regional fora to the PNDC, and to reopen the voters' register clearly underlines the point that the PNDC is bent on continuing to use this body, which is its own creation, and in which Ghanaians have little confidence, to perform the critical function of supervising the elections which will usher Ghana into its future system of government. This is clearly unacceptable, and we reiterate our demand for, and call on all Ghanaians to demand an independent Electoral Commission to replace the PNDC's NCD.

The most fundamental problem with the broadcast, however, is that it seeks to arrogate to the PNDC the right to determine all by itself, and to the exclusion of the people of this country, the crucial processes by which the country is to establish a new constitutional order and democratic government. It is rather the people who must, through their representative organizations, determine what processes the country should go through to bring an end to military rule in the country and usher in democracy. Thus, *what the PNDC should do, in the spirit of "tolerance and reconciliation" is NOT TO DICTATE TO THE WHOLE NATION, but to call a meeting of all organized political forces and independent public organizations at which a real national consensus can be forged on the subsequent phases towards establishing a democratic political system.* At any such meeting, the PNDC would, of course, be free to make whatever *proposals it may have for the consideration of all the parties.*

[ ] We cannot fail to comment on the contradiction between word and deed characteristic of other aspects of the New Year speech. Certainly, we welcome the concern expressed for trade union rights and the rule of law. We cannot however agree with the impression sought to be created that the PNDC has demonstrated in practice such concern. The PNDC's practice and record, as regards trade union rights, show little respect for these rights of workers. This practice includes the arbitrary arrest and detention of workers, the repeated attempts to circumvent the tripartite committee in violation of the law, and other acts, such as the encirclement of the TUC Hall by scores of armed and mounted policemen to prevent the TUC leadership from meeting its members, the workers, in 1987. It was such acts that compelled the 4th Quadrennial Congress of the TUC in 1988 to condemn the repeated violations of trade union rights by the PNDC regime. The recent arbitrary dismissal of the whole junior staff of GHAIP refinery, even as negotiations were in progress between the TUC leaders and high government officials, is further pointer to this anti-democratic practice. In the same vein, the experience of Ghanaians under the PNDC has little to show for the rule of law.

We find especially disturbing the statement that: "the idea of civilian government . . . is a colonial legacy". The attempt to force on Ghanaians the view that the military is the leading political constituency in the country, and has greater responsibility to participate in politics than all other sections of the Ghanaian populace is certainly novel, but it will never be accepted by Ghanaians. While there can be no doubt whatsoever that the military is an integral part of Ghanaian society, such statement smacks of militarism and projects an unfortunate sense of military superiority which has no foundation in real life. Our workers in the mines, doctors and nurses attending to deadly contagious diseases, the farmer who goes to the farm daily and other working people also face the risk of death in service to the nation. Furthermore, it must be clearly stated that *no* worker, teacher or lawyer who enters politics and contests elections does so as a representative of his profession. To think so is to misunderstand the electoral process in national politics.

As an institution, the military does not have one political and social viewpoint; its members have diverse viewpoints. Any soldier who wishes to engage in politics directly is therefore free to do so, but not as a representative of the military as an institution. Above all, to suggest a preponderant role for the military in politics is to attempt to hold a whole nation of 14 million people hostage to some 15,000 men simply because of their monopoly of arms. This has nothing to do with democracy which is premised on the equality of citizens. Fortunately, this is not the position of the great majority of our service personnel who understand their functions and responsibilities in society. It is indeed most regrettable that the PNDC chairman's speech at El-Wak sought to set the military against the rest of the population.

[ ] The vagueness in the wording of important aspects of the New Year broadcast, the lack of any definite time-frame within which the PNDC would be replaced by a duly elected and democratic government, and especially, the continued opposition to multi-party democracy (which a close study of the New Year speech reveals) suggest that the vague promises made are aimed at placating the population and lulling democratic forces into a false sense of security, while the PNDC continues the implementation of its pre-determined programme. All Ghanaians should take note, in this regard, of the statement on New Year day that "The contents of the constitution *we envisage . . . must, as we have always been insisting,* derive from our historical experience and also *the democratic processes set in motion on June 4, 1979 and December 31, 1981*". This clearly shows that the PNDC already has a position on "the contents of the constitution we envisage" which "must" be incorporated in the proposed constitution irrespective of the will of the majority of the people.

In conclusion, we wish to restate, on our own behalf, and in keeping with the expressed positions of the other independent public organizations, our principal demands, and to call on all Ghanaians who cherish a future of peace, national unity and democratic government to step up the pressure on the PNDC to accede to the democratic demands of the population, namely:

1. The PNDC should release immediately all political prisoners and detainees, and grant unconditional amnesty to all political exiles. If even the obnoxious apartheid regime of South Africa has taken certain steps in that direction inside South Africa, it should not be difficult for the PNDC to do the same.
2. The PNDC should repeal immediately all repressive decrees the revocation of which democratic forces have been demanding incessantly: PNDCL 4, PNDCL 91, PNDCL 211, PNDCL 221, and sections of

PNDCL 78 dealing with executions for political offences.
3. An independent Constitutional Committee, made up of representatives of all the major political and other public organizations, as well as of government representation, should be established to begin the work of preparing the draft constitution for the 4th Republic. If such a body should require the services of constitutional experts for drafting the legal wording of the constitutional provisions, the body should appoint the experts after consultations with the relevant legal institutions, such as the Faculty of Law, the Law Reform Commission, the Law School, the Judiciary, and the Attorney General's Department.
4. The draft constitution should be submitted to a Constituent Assembly elected on the basis of universal adult suffrage for discussion, and promulgation.
5. The final programme towards constitutional and democratic government should be the product of a real national consensus arrived at a meeting of all the major independent organizations and the PNDC, and not the dictate of the PNDC. We are therefore calling on the PNDC to call such a meeting now and without any prejudice. [ ]

Signed by:

Johnny F.S. Hansen
(1st Vice Chairman)

Ray Kakraba Quarshie
(2nd National Vice Chairman)

Dan Lartey
(National Treasurer)

Kwesi Pratt, Jnr.
(Deputy National Secretary)

John Ndebugre
(National Organizer)

A. Owusu Gyimah
(Executive Member)

Akoto Ampaw
(Executive Member)

B. K. Nketia
(National Executive Member)

Kwame Wiafe
(Executive Member)

DOCUMENT 11

Evolving a True Democracy: Summary of Memoranda Submitted to the NCD

National Commission for Democracy

The National Commission for Democracy (NCD), was created in 1981. It was charged along with other responsibilities to formulate a programme which would realize true democracy in Ghana. Our history, culture and traditions offer a hitherto untapped alternative to the pre-packaged system with which we have experimented as a nation. The NCD should envisage a new political order which would be rooted in Local Government. This order should demand interaction with a broad spectrum of the people through seminars and workshops and consultations to discover and use their views. The effective representation of people and their active participation at the local level should be the main evidence of true democracy.

Notions of Democracy

Democracy represents the embodiment and achievement of the aspirations of all for a better life, dignified and free. It is characterized by a system of representation that reflects the true and purposeful wishes of the people. Democracy contains that body of principles, attitudes, ideas and orientations which grant human and economic rights and bestow freedom and justice. The question centres on a belief system that is the basis of democracy because it articulates the needs of the entire society. It also outlines the political, spiritual and economic rights of the members of the society which guarantee a truly democratic system of government. Any workable democracy should deal with every unique experience. It ought to, in our peculiar historical condition, begin by decolonizing the mind. Our political parties of the past only gave the appearance of democracy. Indeed, they were weapons for waging economic wars on behalf of specific interest groups. Elections organized along party lines remained political festivals which made available to the elite community the nominal consent of the majority. They succeeded in strengthening the privileges of only the rich who were party founders.

The involvement of the people in decision-making, the formulation and implementation of policies are essential for true democracy. True democracy should transcend political structures to guarantee the welfare of the people. This includes freedom from want, of expression, and a right to the kind of education from which the nation will ultimately benefit. Ghanaian culture provides a basis for deriving a scientific and workable system of government because it is inherently democratic.

Traditional Structures

In some senses our traditional political structures offer us some alternatives to the modern political systems we have known in this country. In spite of some misgivings about its hierarchical nature, the traditional mode which extends from the family at the bottom to the Chief at the top ensures participation and representation at all levels. It is also said to discourage dictatorship. It is a system with built-in checks and balances which make for accountability. It is basically democratic because it ensures most rights, such as the right of association and preserves individual rights. Any future constitution should define a role for Chiefs because they represent the interest of their people.

The Economic Order

The pre-colonial economic system which, it is believed, was free of the exploitation of compatriots and which primarily responded to the basic needs of the society offers a model for a workable economic order. Economic policies must reflect the resources of the country and its political choice. In matters of economics delegation of authority was found to be important. So also was the enforcement of the principles of accountability.

The new constitutional order should review land policies which have been an impediment to economic progress. The vagueness and ambiguity about urban land policies call for the rationalization of land use for residential, commercial and industrial use. A National Land Use Planning Committee should help in achieving the proper consideration of planning at all levels. To this end rural agricultural lands must be registered.

Social Justice

The general mistrust of the legal system by Ghanaians stems from its history of bribes, cronyism, unfair prosecution, crooked judgements, bought juries, prejudiced trials and dehumanizing prison environment. Our legal system appears to resist change. These fears have surfaced because the system ignores our cultural, social and humanistic values. Another area which raises a lot of concern is the mystery in which laws are shrouded. The public must be properly educated about the law. However, the change must go beyond public education. The laws themselves must grow out of the people's experiences and be written in a language which is understood by the people. Customary laws must be reduced to writing and be codified in order to allow for objective referencing.

Constitution

Neither the many Acts which were issued from London during the period of colonial rule nor the constitutions of 1957 and 1969 fully involved the majority of the people in the affairs of the land in the true sense. The 1957, 1969 and 1979 constitutions in theory held out the promise of true democracy. In practice, however, the case was different. A consultative assembly ought to be convened to study all previous constitutions of Ghana alongside the proposals that would emanate from the NCD with a view to finding practical ways to institute a more responsive and participatory type of democracy. A meaningful constitution for this country should draw on the values of the society and ensure an acceptable standard of living for all its citizens.

Politics and Political Parties

The pitfalls of political parties, corruption and general mismanagement, have been attributed to the fact that Independence in Ghana was so rushed that the political parties hardly had time to take roots. The idea of a multi-party system is inherently good, but this system has been abused in Ghana and not been given the opportunity to grow as a result of military interventions. It is felt that an upgrading in civic education should take care of most of the pitfalls of the multi-party system.

Any true system of government should grow out of the people's experience and respond to their aspirations. The search for a new system of government should discourage ideological labels and encourage concrete policies and objectives which respond to the interest of the broad masses of the people.

The socialization of the major means of production and the dispersal of political and economic power through local government are true indices of democratic practice. The District Assemblies which concretize the decentralization of authority would be the highest political and administrative authority in each district. The districts would break down into zones and then into units. An alternative public education programme should help the illiterate in the assembly. Representatives to the Assembly would be chosen on their own merit and there should be a mechanism for monitoring their performance. These representatives should be residents of the community. They must be people who have an interest in the development and welfare of the community. Measures for the recall of Assemblymen will provide built-in checks and balances to ensure justice.

DOCUMENT 12

EXECUTIVE SUMMARY

Regional Seminar on "District Assemblies and the Evolving Democratic Process"

Section 2 (d) (e) of the National Commission for Democracy Law 1988 (PNDCL 208) stipulates that the National Commission for Democracy (NCD) shall:

> formulate for consideration of Government, a programme for a more effective realization of a true democracy in Ghana.

This provision constitutes the constitutional function of the NCD in general terms. Specifically, however, the Blue Book in paragraph 1.7 declares:

> The establishment of District Assemblies is an important step in the PNDC's programme of evolving national political authority through democratic process. The National Commission for Democracy (NCD) has been charged with the responsibility of working out the steps in the programme and also the relationships between the District Assemblies and the ultimate political institutions.

It is in the light of this mandate that the NCD teamed up with the Ministry of Local Government and the Ministry of Information to run the series of regional seminars on "District Assemblies and the Evolving Democratic Process".

The rationale was to invite the views of Ghanaians on "what next after the District Assemblies". This is in fulfillment of the PNDC's intention of not ending the evolution of the country's democratic process at the district level.

The seminars which were held in all the ten regional capitals of the country began in Sunyani on 5 July, and ended at Wa on 9 November, 1990. The executive summary collates the views and ideas expressed at the regional seminars, and presents them under specific headings. It is expected that the report will form the basis for the issue of further directives to the NCD, and that a review of the views and ideas expressed would provide a firm base for the continued interaction with individuals and groups at all levels of the society in order to reach a national consensus on the political framework for the transformation of this country through participatory democracy.

The regional reports present views and ideas expressed in each region separately. All papers read and the formal interventions made by PNDC Members, Regional Secretaries and Chairmen for the seminars are attached as appendices to provide a fuller record of proceedings at each seminar for the benefit of the interested reader.

The keynote address, delivered by the Chairman of the PNDC and Head of State at the very first seminar in Sunyani, and which informed all the subsequent seminars, is presented as preface to the regional reports.

i) There was a deliberate attempt not to weight the views and ideas expressed at the seminars. The primary purpose was to try and capture all views expressed and in doing so to note the nuances indicated in their expression.

ii) However, a review of the views and ideas captured indicate some consensus on the District Assembly concept. The District Assemblies are welcome and the call for their retention and strengthening is clear. So is the desire to make them the cornerstone of the evolving democratic process.

iii) On structures above the District Assemblies, there was the caution that the country makes haste slowly. But the wish for a National Assembly and an Executive Presidency was positively expressed.

iv) A division was discernible on two issues:

   a) in making the District Assemblies the foundation of the new political system, a desire was expressed that nobody should enter the National Assembly except through the District Assemblies. Assembly representatives seemed to wish to monopolize this right. On the other hand, there was a call for universal adult suffrage and the avoidance of any electoral college system.

   b) There was also a sharp division on whether the country should remain non-party or go party. The advocacy for non-party seemed clearly expressed with the phrase "the adoption of the District Assembly concept". The party lobby was united in the call for the introduction of the system. Specifically, however, a division was discernible when some advocates insisted on "only two parties sponsored by the state" others "restricted to three parties", whilst another call was for the reintroduction of a multi-party system.

v) Two different initial stands were discernible in the debate. There were those who took their stand from the fact that there was a Revolution in progress, and that this Revolution had an internal logic of its own, then there were those who seemed to believe that the seminars were an opportunity to start a constitutional discussion afresh.

vi) We submit this report in the conviction that the seminars have been worthwhile and have thrown up ideas which are worthy of consideration, these ideas provide a fulcrum for further discussion and action on "what next after the District Assemblies".

(Sgd.)   E. A. Haizel
(Chief Rapporteur)

Structure Below the District

The PNDC believes that for true democracy to be realized, there should not only be representative of government but also direct structures ouncils and Unit Committees as structures below the District Assemblies.

The Town and Area Councils are yet to be established, but when they are, their main function will be managerial, seeing to it that development programmes in their area of operation are co-ordinated, and providing a means of communication between District Assemblies and Unit Committees, by bringing together Assembly members and Unit Committee members at a single forum. The Unit Committees, made up of ten elected and five appointed members, are to serve a population of 500 to 1,500 people, their functions include:

a) collection of statistics and data which are vital for planning and for the provision of certain amenities;
b) the keeping of records of rateable persons and properties;
c) the provision of assistance in the collection of revenue for District Assemblies and
d) the mobilization of the people for communal labour.

In performing these functions Unit Committees are responsible to District Assemblies through Town or Area Councils. However, Unit Committees also have revolutionary functions, i.e. a commitment to defend the Revolution and its principles of freedom, justice, probity and accountability. When performing these other functions, the Unit Committees are responsible to the higher levels of CDR through the zonal Secretariat.

Issues raised during the seminars concerning structures below the

District Assemblies came mostly in the form of questions and suggestions by participants, and where necessary, answers were given. Most participants who addressed themselves on Town and Area Councils wanted to know when they are to be established and whether they would have the same tenure of office as District Assemblies. The answer given was that Town/Area Councils are soon to be established with a tenure of office of three years. However, the legislative instrument setting up the Councils has transitional provisions to make them serve the remainder of the current term of District Assemblies.

There was also the question as to whether Unit Committees could levy rates or make bye-laws. The answers were that though Unit Committees could ask residents of the units to pay some rates, no sanctions could be brought against defaulters. Such rates could only be enforceable if they were approved by the District Assemblies and given legal backing with bye-laws. Unit Committees were not empowered to make bye-laws. This power is vested only in the District Assemblies. However, Unit Committees could submit proposals to the Assemblies for the enactment of any bye-law. Unit Committees are also not empowered to award contracts. This is a function of District Assemblies which are in turn to consult the District Tender Boards. Unit Committees are however to monitor the execution of such contracts.

There were questions as to how conflicts that arise between Unit Committee and Assembly members at the unit level are to be resolved. The answer was that conflicts need not arise but if they did the traditional system of resolving conflicts which emphasizes reconciliation should be used.

Some participants were of the view that the situation whereby Unit Committees are to be responsible to both the District Assemblies and CDR is a source of potential conflict since, as they put it, "no person can serve two masters at the same time".

The demand for the establishment of the structures below the district level without further delay and in order to strengthen the District Assemblies came up at every seminar. It was felt that elections to select members of the Unit Committees should be conducted by the NCD instead of the CDR.

District Level

A great majority of participants expressed the view that the District Assembly concept is very laudable and should be made the foundation on which any future political system is based. The following suggestions were, however, made to improve upon the practice of the concept:

a) adequate allowances should be paid to Assembly members;
b) the Central Government should bear the payment of the salaries of workers of District Assemblies in full;
c) membership of the Assemblies should be reduced. This could be done by the reduction either of the number of appointed members or of the electoral areas. Some participants were of the view that the three-year tenure of office of Assembly members is too short and should therefore be increased to four or five years. Others, however, thought that three years is enough.

Another issue was the mode of appointment of PNDC District Secretaries. Some argued that because District Secretaries are appointed by the PNDC they do not feel a part of the District Assemblies and most times ignore them. Two suggestions emerged as solutions:

a) District Secretaries should be elected by the Assemblies/Communities.
b) District Secretaries should be appointed by the PNDC in consultation with the members of District Assemblies.

Some participants, however, were of the opinion that the present system of appointment be retained. The position of the Presiding Member came up for debate. There appeared some dissatisfaction with the role assigned to the Presiding Member. Views expressed were that the Presiding Member should not be limited to presiding over meetings of the Assembly only. He could become a member of the other committees of the Assembly. Indeed, there was a suggestion that he should chair the Executive Committee of the Assembly as well.

It was also suggested that the tenure of office of the Presiding Member and the Executive Committee should be increased from the present one year to three years to coincide with the tenure of office of Assembly members.

Participants also called for a vigorous pursuit of the policy of decentralization in order to make the District Assemblies effective, especially the transfer of means and know-how and the provision of adequate infrastructure.

There was a strong feeling that the office of the Ombudsman should be decentralized to the districts so as to deal with:

a) resolution of conflicts between District Secretaries and Presiding Members; and
b) complaints about maladministration on the part of District Assemblies and any of their committees.

It was agreed that there is the need to take another look at teacher-Assembly members and the effect of their political work on their pupils.

There was a suggestion that the Attorney-General's office should be made responsible for the approval of District Assembly bye-laws instead of the Ministry of Local Government.

It was suggested that Organs of the Revolution in the Districts should be answerable to the District Assemblies. Other issues raised were:
a) review of PNDCL 207 to make it more functional.
b) re-introduction of the Local Government Grants Commission
c) establishment of a Local Government Service distinct from the Civil Service.

Regional Level

The view was expressed that the Regional Co-ordinating Councils (RCCs) and their functions as presently defined should be retained. The main reason offered for keeping the RCC's in their present form was to forestall any tendency towards regionalism or federalism which most participants contended would not augur well for Ghana.

It is, however, necessary to place on record that a contrary view was raised in the Western region where a range of speakers advocated strongly for a Regional Assembly. It was argued that the region lagged behind all other regions in infrastructural development in spite of its being a major contributor to the country's wealth. It was therefore contended that a Regional Assembly could champion the cause for an equitable distribution of the national cake better than the present arrangements.

There was a suggestion that the name of Regional Co-ordinating Councils should be changed to Regional Assemblies but with the current functions retained.

A further suggestion in this line of thinking was for the RCCs to revert to Regional Consultative Councils but with an expanded membership and the right to elect its own chairman.

A completely different view was for the establishment of a Regional Assembly, members of which, including the Regional Secretaries, were to be elected and on party lines.

A number of divergent views were expressed on the composition of the RCCs. The following suggestions were made:
i) chiefs to be given a place on the Regional Co-ordinating Councils.
ii) membership to include representatives of identifiable groups and regional directors of departments.
iii) an additional member from each of the District Assemblies to make the representation three;
iv) an addition of two members from each of the District Assemblies;

v) there should be three members from each district made up of the Presiding Member and two others elected from the District Assembly (thus leaving out the District Secretary)

vi) district representation should be four comprising the Presiding Members, the District Secretary, the District Organizing Assistant of CDR and a representative of the Traditional Council

vii) two more District Assembly members from each district and five representatives from the Regional House of Chiefs.

Other areas on which suggestions were made include the following:

i) that Regional Co-ordinating Councils should run for a five-year term;

ii) that each Regional Co-ordinating Council is to elect its own chairman with the Regional Secretary as an ex-officio member.

National Structures

The Executive

There was consensus on the need to have an Executive Presidency. However, there were differences in opinion on the eligibility, mode of election and tenure of office of the president.

i) Eligibility: Suggestions made on eligibility of individuals for the post of President include:

    a) an age range of 40-70 years

    b) membership of the National Assembly

    c) any Ghanaian of at least 40 years

    d) where the President is a man, the Vice should be a woman

    e) where the President is from the South, the vice should come from the North.

ii) Mode of Election:

    a) the National Assembly should elect the President from amongst themselves

    b) the National Assembly should elect the President either from within or without the Assembly

    c) the National Assembly to nominate a specified number of candidates from within or without the Assembly to be voted for by universal adult suffrage

    d) the National Commission for Democracy to screen and present a specified number of candidates to be voted for by universal adult suffrage

e) political parties should be formed for the purpose of presidential elections
   f) District Assemblies to serve as electoral colleges and elect a President from candidates nominated by the NCD.
iii) Tenure of Office: A tenure of office of three (3) to five (5) years for a maximum of two (2) terms was suggested.

The PNDC

Specific views on the PNDC vis-a-vis the Executive were as follows:

(i) the PNDC should be redesignated the National Defence Council to exercise executive powers with one of the members as President
ii) the PNDC to remain as an executive body but with an enlarged membership.
iii) Chairman of the PNDC to be the first Executive President
iv) the PNDC to be in power to supervise the new democratic process as a transitional measure
v) the PNDC to come out with a time-table for a return to constitutional rule
vi) suggestions as to the time-frame when PNDC should fold up were offered:
   a) September 1991
   b) September 1993
   c) the end of two terms after the inception of the National Assembly.

Council of State

i) There was a suggestion for the establishment of a body to advise the President. Various names suggested for such a body were:
   a) Council of State
   b) National Defence Council
   c) House of Elders
   d) National Political Advisory Council
ii) Proposals on its composition were:
   a) commanders of the Army, Navy, Air Force, IGP, Head of Civil Service, TUC, National House of Chiefs and other identifiable bodies;
   b) head of security services and Revolutionary Organs;
   c) a representative from each region;
   d) group of eminent citizens;

    e) all former Heads of State
    f) all former Chief Justices.

Judiciary

i) There was consensus on the need to guarantee the independence of the Judiciary;
ii) On the dual judicial system, views expressed were as follows:
   a) a merger of the traditional courts and the tribunals;
   b) the two systems to stay in their present form;
   c) the two systems to remain separate at the lower levels but have a common Appeal Court.

Legislature

There was overwhelming consensus for a National Assembly. Submissions, however, differed on the mode of election, composition and tenure of office. Concrete proposals on the National Assembly and how it is to be formed are as follows:

i) *Unicameral Legislature on Non-Party Lines*
   a) A specified number of representatives elected by each District Assembly from its membership.
   b) A specified number of representatives elected by each District Assembly from within or without the Assembly.
   c) Representatives from districts nominated from District Assemblies and elected by the people.
   d) Representatives from the district, nominated from within or outside the District Assemblies and elected by popular vote.
   e) Elected representatives from the districts and a specified number of representatives of identifiable groups.
   f) Representatives from Regional Co-ordinating Councils and members of identifiable groups and opinion leaders appointed by PNDC.
   g) Two-thirds of membership elected by District Assemblies from their membership and a third appointed by PNDC from within or outside the District Assemblies.

(ii) *Bicameral Legislature*

   a) A bicameral legislature with a Lower House elected by adult suffrage on non-party basis, and the Upper House made up

of eminent citizens and representatives of identifiable groups.
b) A bicameral legislature with Lower House elected on party lines, and the Upper House comprising eminent citizens and representatives of identifiable groups.

iii) There was advocacy for elections on party lines on one hand, and on the other, the avoidance of any electoral college system. Elections should be by universal adult suffrage.

iv) Suggestions for the tenure of office of the National Assembly ranged from three to five years. As to when to introduce the National Assembly, one view was that the District Assemblies must be improved qualitatively before the imposition of any superstructure. Should the need arise, the District Assemblies and the National Political Advisory Council to be established would be called upon to elect an Interim Government and its President. Another view was that, we should move ahead and use the 1979 constitution, with the addition of District Assemblies, as a basis.

Revolutionary Organs

Ideas expressed on Revolutionary Organs were as follows:

i) The revolutionary Organs must be strengthened to play the role of of conscientizing the masses and mobilizing them for socio-economic development.

ii) The CDR must be allowed to collect market and lorry station tolls tolls for a commission to enable them run their secretariat.

iii) Abolition of CDO and CDR in the event of the exit of the PNDC. However, 31st December Women's Movement is to be maintained with a change in name.

iv) A merger of all Revolutionary Organs to be redesignated Committee for the Defence of the State to handle:
   a) civic education;
   b) youth mobilization

v) A scrutiny of the personnel within the CDR.

National Commission for Democracy

i) A reconstitution of the Commission was suggested. Two ideas came up:
   a) regional representation
   b) representatives of interest groups

ii) Impartiality of the Commission was doubted by some participants so far as the outcome of the consultations on the country's political future is concerned. The reason given for this fear is the chairmanship of the Commission by a PNDC Member. There was therefore a call for an outside body to conduct a referendum, should the need arise.

iii) Another suggestion was that the Commission should be strengthened to discharge all its responsibilities efficiently.

iv) The Voters Register should be reopened and residual demarcation issues settled.

v) Citizens identity cards should be issued as a matter of priority.

vi) The seminars on the country's political future should be extended to the districts, markets, schools and institutions at the same time as political education is intensified.

Partisan and Non-Partisan Politics

The issue of pluralism in the evolving democratic process was one which generated the most heat, and showed a clear divide in the opinion of participants.

i) One group, made up predominantly of representatives from District Assemblies and an appreciable number of other bodies and individuals stated categorically that party politics had had its chance and failed, and therefore should not be allowed to return into the political fibre of the country. The main arguments used to support this stand were that:

a) party politics in this country has had the tendency of dividing the populace into opposing groups leading to strife and bloodshed. The proponents of this argument used the CPP-NLM era as a case in point and pointed out that if party politics were reintroduced into the country, such animosity and violence could not be ruled out;

b) party politics has led to the reinforcement of tribalism. Our political history has shown that membership of political parties and the casting of votes for the political parties have most of the time followed tribal lines, undermining nation-building in the process. Thus the NAL was typically pro-Ewe and the PP was pro-Akan;

c) party politics has bred corruption. The funding of political parties by individuals and organizations has in most cases been perceived as a profit-making venture. The parties were indeed limited liability companies. This situation led in the past to a situation where winning parties concentrated on how to pay back loans

or recoup expenses on elections;
d) further because of foreign sources of funding, party politics undermined allegiance to the state; and
e) generally party politics with its opposition is alien to the ethos of our society.

Their conclusion therefore was that there should not be party politics in the country.

ii) A second view was that party politics could work in this country provided certain guarantees were put in place. These include:
   a) formation and funding of parties by the state;
   b) restriction of the number of parties to two or three. There were suggestions to the effect that there have been only two political traditions in the country — the CPP and PP traditions. However, with June 4th and 31st December, there has evolved a third tradition, and the PNDC and its organs should therefore constitute a third party.
   c) one guarantee to make parties work was that there should be a limit to the amount of money that any group or individual could contribute to the formation and running of a party.

iii) The third view that emerged was that there was nothing wrong with party politics *per se* and therefore it should be reintroduced. The proponents of this view stated amongst others that:
   a) one-party and military regimes have not allowed for opposition, thus leading to the rule of the few
   b) the argument that party politics has failed the country is false and that in all the 33 years of independence in this country Ghanaians have had less than ten years of multi-party rule. The rest of the period has been for one-party or military regimes. Therefore party politics could not be responsible for the woes of our society;
   c) furthermore the military had not allowed the parties in power to find their feet before they intervened, whilst the military and one-party regimes have stayed longer because of their ability to intimidate the people;
   d) the one-party system and the military regimes have not fared any better than the multi-party system.

iv) A variant on the view to reintroduce party politics was that although there should be party politics it should be limited to elections to the National Assembly and the Presidency. Any structure below these should be contested for on a non-party basis, and on the personal merit of candidates.

v) A further variant wanted party politics limited to the election of the president only.

vi) There was also the view that the present decentralization programme with the establishment of the District Assemblies is not incompatible with any type of system we decide to adopt, be it non-party, one-party or multi-party. The options should therefore remain open.

Identifiable Groups

i) There was a persistent call for the institutional involvement of identifiable groups in the political life of the country. However, there was opposition to this view on the ground that everybody belonged to a district which should provide a political base.

ii) There was difficulty in the articulation of what the identifiable groups are. However, names like the TUC, Ghana Bar Association, Christian Council, Catholic Secretariat, Muslim Council, Ghana Journalists Association, NUGS, the Universities, Security Services, and the House of Chiefs came in for regular mention. Meanwhile, there were present at the seminars other groups such as the Butchers Association, Chop-Bar Keepers Association, Garage Owners Association and Market Women's Association.

iii) The involvement of identifiable groups is to be concentrated at the regional and national levels. At the regional level, there were calls for the expansion of Regional Co-ordinating Councils to include representatives of specified identifiable groups. At the national level, the idea which emerged was either a unicameral legislature comprising both elected representatives and representatives of identifiable groups or a bicameral legislature with the Lower House elected and the Upper House comprising representatives of identifiable groups.

iv) There were also calls to the effect that sensitive organs of state such as the National Commission for Democracy and the Press Commission should be composed of representatives of identifiable groups.

v) Lectures delivered at the seminar on "Traditional Ghanaians System of Government and the Evolving Democratic Process" provoked an interesting discussion on the role of chieftaincy in the evolving system.

By the end of the regional seminars, three schools of thought had emerged:

a) the institution of chieftaincy should be restricted to its traditional role because there is no example of a modern national state based

on traditional authority;
   b) a critical study of the institution with a view to adopting its progressive elements in our national life;
   c) representative of chiefs at all levels of government.
vi) specific roles suggested for chiefs among others were:
   a) the next President be called Paramount Chief of Ghana and be elected by the National House of Chiefs on regional basis;
   b) the name Republic of Ghana be changed to Chiefdom of Ghana;
   c) empowerment of traditional councils to try civil in addition to chieftaincy cases;
   d) traditional councils should be allowed to establish and maintain their own police force;
   e) a National Advisory Council comprising Presidents of Regional Houses of Chiefs to advise the President;
   f) a National Council of Elders comprising chiefs and representatives of other groups to advise the Executive President;
   g) the National House of Chiefs to send representatives to the National Assembly;
   h) representatives from Regional House of Chiefs to join Regional Co-ordinating Councils;
   i) traditional rulers to send direct representatives to the District Assemblies;
   j) regional and district political heads be appointed in consultation with traditional rulers;
   k) traditional rulers to have a say in the appointment of the one-third Unit Committee members in their localities;
   l) traditional rulers in consultation with Unit Committees to periodically organize fora to assess performance of Assembly members;
   m) an electoral college comprising representatives of the traditional councils, Revolutionary Organs and identifiable groups to elect representatives from the district to the National Assembly;
   n) a Chieftaincy Commission insulated from direct government control to handle all matters pertaining to chieftaincy in the country.
vii) The role of the military in whatever political system evolved provoked an interesting discussion at all the regional seminars.
viii) A preoccupation with the survival of the country's future political arrangement brought into focus the question of the abrupt interruptions of constitutionally elected governments in the past.
ix) The focus was, however, not on the justification or otherwise of

the previous military interventions but on the creation of an atmosphere that would make resort to arms to overthrow a constitutional government look unattractive and unnecessary.

x) Three main ideas came up with regard to the role of the military in any future political system:
   a) the military as an institution should be scrapped;
   b) the military should be taken through a comprehensive orientation programme after a return to civilian rule so as to respect the sanctity of a constitutional government.
   c) the military has now become a major power bloc and is therefore a *de facto* political constituency. Future systems of government should therefore shift from the traditional civilian-military cooperation which emphasized the traditional military role of defence to civilian-military integration which emphasizes the indispensability of the military in the political administration of the country.

xi) Specific proposals as to the concretization of military involvement in politics were:
   a) if the President is a civilian, his deputy should be a soldier and *vice versa*;
   b) representatives of identifiable groups including the military to join the National Assembly;
   c) a National Security Council comprising Service Commanders and other security heads to handle security in this country; and
   d) a Council of State comprising representatives of the military and other identifiable groups to advise the President.

Referendum

(i) Specific calls for a referendum of a sort were heard in all the regions except one. Proponents of referendum cut across a wide spectrum of individuals and organizations including students, chiefs, District Assemblies and professional bodies, but it was clear that proponents did not have a common position on the issue(s) to be decided on at a referendum. While some talked of a straight decision between multi-party and non-party systems of government, others called for a referendum on the continued stay in office of the PNDC.

ii) A school of thought was that the Government should work out a constitutional package for Ghanaians to either accept or reject at a referendum.

iii) It was also argued that no constitution should be introduced into this country unless it was agreed upon at a referendum.

iv) The NCD was also tasked to draft a constitution on the basis of discussions at the regional seminars and other submissions by identifiable groups and to subject such a document to study and finally to a referendum.

v) To a participant at Takoradi, a referendum is the only acceptable means of determining the wishes of Ghanaians on the country's political future and unless this is done, any other declaration by the NCD would be a farce.

vi) Another suggestion was for a referendum based on the theme for the regional seminars viz: "District Assemblies and the Evolving Democratic Process" because the Assemblies are a viable part of the evolving process.

viii) It was also discernible that some people asked for a referendum without any thought to the issue(s) to be raised. There was a seeming contradiction on the part of certain contributors who did not merely ask for a referendum on the country's political future, but also suggested for outright adoption, specific systems of administration.

ix) In reaction to the calls for a referendum it was stated that the PNDC does not have anything against a referendum *per se*. However, its necessity or the issues to be raised could not be objectively determined until the NCD has finished with the sampling of the opinion of Ghanaians on the future political system of the country.

x) There were divided positions as to which agency or organization should conduct and/or supervise a national referendum should the need arise.

xi) Whereas the conduct of referenda is part of the statutory functions of the National Commission for Democracy, a few contributors expressed their apprehension about the ability of the National Com mission for Democracy in conducting a fair referendum. This is because the NCD was constituted by the PNDC which is not a disinterested party so far as the political future of this country is concerned. Moreover the Chairman of the NCD is a member of the PNDC.

xii) Specific suggestions made to address the above concern were:

   a) a Monitoring Team from the ECOWAS Secretariat or the UN to handle any referendum; and

   b) the NCD as presently constituted be dissolved and be recomposed with representatives of identifiable social and political groups before any referendum is held. There was, however,

another view that the NCD as presently constituted should conduct a referendum should it become necessary so to do.

Miscellaneous

A number of general views were expressed. Among these are:
i) a written constitution expressing the sovereign will of the people and guaranteeing fundamental human rights, separation of powers, rule of law, independence of the judiciary, press freedom, accountability and probity in public life, social justice, national unity and progress;
ii) intensification of public education and reintroduction of the Ideological Institute if necessary. In addition there should be a programme of awareness such that Ghanaians will resist any attempt at overthrowing a post-PNDC government, by recourse to civil disobedience;
iii) equitable distribution of national resources and development projects, and the fostering of national unity through appointments to diplomatic and political positions, recruitment into the security services; admissions into the universities and the award of scholarships;
iv) free flow of information to the people, and the establishment of a Press Commission;
v) a Constituent Assembly composed of chiefs, workers, the military, the police, etc. to draw up an appropriate constitution for the country.
vi) development and improvement of the concept of civil defence to include military training for all Ghanaians above eighteen years.
vii) the new political system to guarantee fee-free education to all children up to at least the JSS level, and the intensification of the functional literacy drive and introduction of special educational schemes for the Northern Sector of the country.
viii) the need to address the question of career administration without which no political system can function effectively; and
ix) the recognition that true democracy can only succeed on a strong economic foundation, but that it takes a democratic process to sustain economic development.
x) the repeal of:
   i) PNDC L -4 — Preventive Custody
   ii) PNDC L 78 — Public Tribunals

  iii) PNDC L 91 — Habeas Corpus
  iv)   " 211 — Newspaper Licensing
  v)   " 244 — Religious Bodies;

xi) release of all political prisoners from protective custody and a general amnesty for all political refugees;

xii) a Press Commission comprising representatives of identifiable groups.

xiii) abolition of Civil Defence Organization, Bureau of National Investigations and the Personal Security Corps.

DOCUMENT 13

Government's Statement on the NCD Report on Evolving True Democracy

On 25 March, 1991, the National Commission for Democracy (NCD) presented to the Government its report on "Evolving True Democracy". The report summarizes the work of the NCD as the body set up in 1982 to perform the dual functions of an Electoral Commission and also to assist in developing a programme for a more effective realization of democracy in Ghana.

The NCD also played a major part in the establishment of District Assemblies and their sub-structures as the institutional framework for decentralized administration and development, and has been providing a framework for increased and effective civic and political education.

The consultative processes engaged in by the NCD, climaxed by the Regional Seminars on "district assemblies and the evolving democratic process" led to the articulation by Ghanaians of all walks of life of their major concerns for the future governance of the country.

These concerns are enumerated in the NCD Report's chapter on "Main Issues for Consideration by the Consultative Assembly".

The main issues include human rights particularly workers' rights, women's rights, children's rights, and the rights of the handicapped. They also include the basic freedoms of speech, of conscience, of assembly and association, freedom from arbitrary arrest and detention, and also from invasion of privacy.

The NCD report addressed issues of representation and the need for ensuring that language is not a barrier to genuine popular participation in government. Accountability and responsibility are both stressed in the report; the former by insisting that a Code of Conduct for high office holders be included in the next Constitution, and the latter by suggesting that aspiring office holders must have fulfilled all their tax obligations, and also that specific constitutional duties be imposed on National Assemblymen and high political office holders.

The report notes that Ghanaians see the existence of political parties as an expression of the fundamental freedom of association, but that the operation of future political parties should be shown of the excesses and iniquities of the past.. It is proposed that provision be made in the Constitution to guard against such abuses.

A wide-ranging set of issues are put on the agenda for the Consultative Assembly by the NCD including also the nature, functions and power of the various organs of State, such as the National Assembly, the Executive, the Judiciary and the security agencies, and a re-examination of our citizenship laws.

A strengthened Ombudsman as a more functional agency in the redress of executive and administrative excesses and of maladministration at both national and district levels is discussed.

The NCD report further identifies positive achievements already made in the area of participatory democracy but which require to be constitutionally underwritten in the new framework of national administration. These include participatory democracy at the local level, represented by the district assemblies and their sub-structures; decentralized administration for development; revenue-sharing between Central Government and local authorities; accountability of candidates and elected officials to their electorate both before and after elections, with the possibility of recall in case of default; as well as a framework for monitoring and assessing the performance of elected officials.

Government has studied the report and accepts the various views expressed as the embodiment of the aspirations of Ghanaians on the future constitutional order, and will accordingly submit the report to the Consultative Assembly as one of the major source documents for its deliberations. Government will formulate constitutional proposals to be placed before the Consultative Assembly which will reflect the concerns that have been articulated in the report. Accordingly Government has decided to set up a Committee made up of Constitutional experts which will begin to formulate these proposals.

The Committee will be under the chairmanship of Dr. S.K.B. Asante, a former Solicitor-General and currently a Director of the United Nations Centre for Transnational Corporations. The services of the Committee will also be available to the Consultative Assembly.

The constitutional proposals will make provision for freedom of association, including the formation of political parties. There will also be provision for independent candidates. Although during the consultative processes of the NCD there was a substantial body opinion expressing concern about the past conduct of political parties, the NCD report points the way to making constitutional provisions to guard against such abuse.

Ultimately it will be the responsibility of all Ghanaians to ensure the proper functioning of any institutions that are provided for under the Constitution.

The constitutional proposals will make provision for an Executive President to be elected on the basis of universal adult suffrage.

Provision will also be made for a Prime Minister who must command a majority in the National Assembly. Elections to the National Assembly will also be on the basis of universal adult suffrage.

As the need for national consensus on critical national issues has been highlighted by the NCD report, the proposals will embody forms of co-operation between political parties, National Assembly Members and other institutions to define in an ongoing manner the areas of consensus on which partisan considerations can be muted in the supreme interest of the nation.

In this regard, the proposals will provide for certain institutions and constitutional functions to remain above partisan politics. Such institutions and functions must include the Judiciary and the Military.

The proposal will also make provision for other areas of non-partisanship in which persons will serve without reference to party affiliation. Such institutions can provide a context in which chiefs, elder statesmen, military personnel etc. can contribute their views to deliberations on national affairs in a manner that transcends partisan consideration. The exact form of such institutions will require detailed consideration in the Consultative Assembly.

The NCD report indicates consensus that district assembly elections continue to be held on a non-party basis with candidates standing on their individual merit and not under the sponsorship of a political party. The constitutional proposals will reflect this consensus and will clarify the relationship between the functions of the District Assembly and the National Assembly.

The constitutional proposals will also reflect the following:

— a commitment to fundamental human rights and basic freedoms, including workers' and trade union rights, women's rights, including the rights of widows provided for in the Intestate Succession Law, children's rights especially against child abuse, the rights of the handicapped and disadvantaged minorities, freedom of speech, freedom from arbitrary arrest and detention and from invasion of privacy, and freedom of assembly and association. In addition, there should be a mechanism in the Constitution for the enforcement and protection of these fundamental liberties;
— constitutional guarantees of the Legal Aid Scheme, and the Office of the Ombudsman;
— a free independent and incorruptible Judiciary;

— the freedom and independence of the media;
— a decentralized system of national administration, based on a virile local government system with development as its objective, and including revenue-sharing clauses;
— a commitment to equal and balanced development in the allocation of national resources and in the distribution of the national wealth.

The NCD report touched briefly on the importance of the economic foundations for evolving a true democracy. It is perhaps unfortunate that they considered the issue of the economy as not strictly within the mandate of the NCD and, therefore, did not elaborate on this.

There is no doubt that the continued improvement of the national economy is a necessity for ensuring the stability of the new constitutional order. There can also be no doubt that the modest but important gains that have been made in the economy would need to be consolidated and the directions of the Economic Recovery Programme continued to enable further improvements to be made in the lives of ordinary people.

Accordingly, as has been exemplified many times in many Western democracies, in times of national crisis and transition, a national must be developed regarding the direction of economic growth. This will ensure that Ghana continues to receive the much-needed assistance from the international community in the pursuit of our national reconstruction.

Accordingly, the pertinent issues relating to the national economy and measures to sustain and enhance it will be placed before the Consultative Assembly for deliberation.

A law establishing the Consultative Assembly will be published next week and the Consultative Assembly will begin its deliberations in July this year.

The Consultative Assembly will be composed of elected representatives of District Assemblies, identifiable bodies and appointed persons in accordance with previous practice in 1968 and 1978.

In accordance with such the Government recognizes that the process of constitutional deliberation should be non-partisan and, therefore, the ban on political parties will remain for the time being.

The draft constitution will be to the people of Ghana for their approval in a national referendum. As part of the arrangements towards the new constitutional order and in the light of the recommendations made in the NCD report, the government will take steps to reorganize and reconstitute the NCD to enable the Commission to fully discharge its electoral as well as its civil education functions.

The success of our democratic processes will depend on the mature conduct of all Ghanaians. To establish a solid basis for constitutional democracy that can stand the test of time, we must all take lessons from the past and work in the national interest to achieve our national aspirations.

DOCUMENT 14

Statement by the Movement for Freedom and Justice (MFJ) on the PNDC'S Statement on the "NCD Report and the Constitutional Proposals" Accra, 17, May 1991

Ghana is at the political crossroads, and we have called you here this morning to convey, through you, to the people of Ghana and the world community the position of the Movement for Freedom and Justice (MFJ) on the recent statement of the PNDC on the NCD Report and the so-called "constitutional proposals" which seek to make far-reaching decisions on the country's future system of government without reference to the sovereign people of Ghana.

Since the PNDC initiated its so-called "national discussion on the political future of the country" on 5 July 1990, two basic positions have emerged on the political scene: the multi-party democracy stance based on fundamental human rights, and the no-party system which is nothing but a continuation of the existing dictatorship. While all the major independent public organizations and the overwhelming majority of Ghanaians opted for multi-party democracy, the PNDC and its organs of rule, especially its District Assemblies, took a determined position against multi-partyism in favour of a no-party system. With growing pressure from the democratic movement in the country, however, the regime began to shift its position. First, it declared that it had not taken a position against multi-party democracy, and that it would abide by whatever choice the people made. Then under greater pressure, it began to make ambivalent concessions in favour of multi-party democracy, while manoeuvering to find a way of imposing its hidden agenda on the people behind the veil of manipulatory rhetoric. The 10 May statement of the PNDC on the NCD Report crowns this policy of containment and manipulation.

[ ] Since 5 July, the people of this country, through their representative and independent public organizations, have consistently made known their positions on the political future of the country in various policy statements and memoranda, and at numerous public meetings and fora. These positions and aspirations of the people have, over time, become compressed into SEVEN BASIC DEMANDS. To appreciate the full import of the government statement, therefore, it is necessary to compare the positions and proposals contained in it with the SEVEN BASIC DEMANDS

of the people for multi-party democracy and respect for fundamental human rights.

1. The people have consistently demanded the *immediate* lifting of the ban on party political activity; the PNDC has however decreed, in its statement of 10 May that the ban on the formation of political parties will remain till some indefinite and unknown date in the future. Meanwhile the PNDC is going about organizing its own forces forces with public funds and by state patronage.

2. The people have persistently demanded the *immediate* repeal of all repressive laws in the country, particularly the Preventive Custody Law, the Habeas Corpus Amendment Law, the Newspaper Licensing Law, the Religious Bodies (Registration) Law, and sections of PNDCL 78 dealing with executions for political offences. This demand has persistently been made by the democratic movement with the aim of creating an atmosphere of openness and freedom devoid of the fear and intimidation imposed on the country by the PNDC so that all Ghanaians can freely participate in shaping their future system of government. If the PNDC were sincere, it should have no problem with meeting this elementary demand. The PNDC has, however, simply evaded this demand by the vague statement that existing laws will be reviewed to bring them into conformity with provisions on human rights in the future constitution. But if the PNDC 'white paper' of 10 May recognizes that "freedom of speech, freedom from arbitrary arrest and detention and from invasion of privacy" are fundamental human rights that must be enshrined in the future constitution, then the PNDC should have no reason for maintaining these oppressive laws on our statute books, even today.

3. 'Ghanaians have demanded the *immediate* release of all political prisoners and detainees languishing in jail under the PNDC; the PNDC has callously refused to accede to this humane and democratic demand which even the obnoxious apartheid regime of South Africa is beginning to heed.

4. The people have demanded unconditional amnesty for all Ghanaians driven into political exile by the repression and the intimidatory tactics of the PNDC; the regime treats this important demand with contempt by ignoring it completely.

5. Ghanaians have demanded the dissolution of the PNDC's NCD and its replacement by an independent electoral commission made up of representatives from independent public organizations, such as the TUC, the GNAT, the NUGS, the Muslim Council, the Christian Council of Ghana, the Catholic Bishops' Conference, farmers' and fishermen's

associations, women and the professional bodies, and to be headed by a judge of the superior court of justice. The PNDC has tried to side-step this specific demand by its unilateral and vague decision to "reorganize and reconstitute the NCD". This is completely unsatisfactory for it leaves intact the sinister 'political education' function of the NCD and allows the regime to determine, once again, the composition of this body.

6. The people have called for an independent and representative constitutional conference, made up of all the independent public organizations and other political forces and organizations, to map out a clear and definite time-table for the return to democratic government, and to draw up a draft constitution; the PNDC has completely ignored this demand and has refused even to propose a time-table for handing over to a duly elected government. Instead, the regime, in bad faith, has been trying to buy time for itself through its piecemeal pronouncements on its stage-managed "evolving democratic process".

7. The people have demanded the convocation of a constituent assembly, elected by universal adult suffrage from the hundred and forty (140) constituencies of old, to discuss and amend the draft constitution, and to promulgate the constitution of the Fourth Republic. The PNDC has contemptuously ignored this and is in the process of imposing its own consultative body on the country.

[ ] This is DICTATORSHIP, not democracy. The PNDC has simply decided to ignore these basic demands of the population and to pursue its pre-determined constitutional programme with minor concessions to contain popular demands and deceive the people. We are confident, however, that Ghanaians will not be deceived by such manoeuvres.

The *fundamental question* that the PNDC's statement on the NCD Report raises, however, is *whether the PNDC has the right to determine, to the exclusion of the people of Ghana, the processes by which Ghanaians establish a democratic system of government and the form of government they want. It is only the people themselves who have the sovereign right to take such vital decisions affecting their destiny.* Contrary to this, the PNDC has been "composing its own tune and dancing to only that tune", and this is precisely what it is trying to do again with its statement on the NCD Report.

The PNDC has decided, all by itself, to establish a "national consultative body" the composition of which it has determined without reference to Ghanaians. It is obvious from the decreed modalities for its composition that the "national consultative body" will be packed with at least a hundred and ten (110) representatives from the PNDC's district assemblies. Ghanaians will recollect that during the NCD-organized fora, almost every single District Assembly just recited, by note, identical litanies against multi-party democracy, and called for the bankrupt no-party system. This already showed that the district assemblies were being manipulated by an external force, the PNDC. By packing the proposed consultative body with district assembly members and PNDC appointees, the PNDC clearly intends to exercise total control over the deliberations and decisions of the body. The inclusion of "identifiable bodies" in the membership of the consultative body is a transparent attempt to give a cloak of legitimacy to an illegitimate creation of the PNDC. No matter what number of representatives, the independent public organizations may be allowed by the pleasure of the PNDC, they will still be completely outnumbered by PNDC loyalists from the District Assemblies and other PNDC appointees. This once more exposes the bad faith of the regime. How can district assemblies that are opposed to multi-party democracy convene to fashion a multi-party constitution?

The PNDC is not only bent on dictating the processes and mechanism by which a new constitutional order is to be established; it is also determined to dictate to a population of over fourteen (14) million even the very contents of the future constitution. Thus, even before its self-created consultative body begins to sit, the PNDC has formulated 'constitutional proposals' which are bound to set the pace and tone of deliberations for the consultative body. If one also considers the composition of the consultative body, there can be no doubt that the PNDC is seeking to determine in advance the structure of Ghana's future system of government. This includes the idea of an executive president, a prime minister commanding the majority in the future national assembly, various questionable restrictions on the operation of political parties, and the attempt to entrench the PNDC's economic programme in the future constitution.

This is wholly unacceptable. In the view of the MFJ, it is irrelevant, at this stage, whether Ghanaians will arrive at some or all of these proposals by themselves. What is important is that the PNDC has no right to arrogate to itself the determination of what system of government is good for Ghanaians. This is the sovereign right of the people.

We wish, at this stage, to make some comments on the 'constitutional proposals' themselves.

First, though the PNDC statement suggests that the freedom of association, including the freedom to form political parties of one's choice, has, at long last, been recognized, a close study of the statement and the NCD report shows that this freedom will be so restricted as to be seriously undermined.

One such restriction on the right to free association is the idea of limiting the number of parties Ghanaians may form to only two or three. This, in our view, constitutes a complete negation of the freedom of association. Ghanaians should be free to form whatever number of parties they so desire without any constitutional or legislative limitation.

Another problem is the decision of the PNDC to further restrict the freedom of association by confining political parties to only the "national level". We see this as a clear manifestation of the PNDC's residual hostility to political parties. It is also a surreptitious attempt to preserve the PNDC's District Assemblies in the future constitution. No Ghanaian lives only at the "national level". Indeed, all Ghanaians live in the districts and the communities. To say therefore that politics at the national level will be partisan but will be non-partisan at the district level is a poor pretence since people living in the districts will necessarily belong to parties.

Even more serious is the decision to impose, at the national level, the so-called "innovation in the District Level Elections . . . of creating a common platform for all candidates to present themselves and their programmes to the electorate" (see NCD Report, pages 35 to 36). This decision is a gross violation not only of the freedom of association, but of the freedom of assembly and speech as well, and it must be completely rejected together with the other undemocratic restrictions on the right to form parties.

Another disturbing feature of the PNDC 'white paper' on the NCD report is the plan to impose the PNDC's district assembly system on Ghanaians as a system representative of the will of the people. The MFJ has already made known its position on the district assembly system and we need not elaborate it here. Suffice it to say that, though there are many honest and patriotic Ghanaians in the district assemblies, the system itself was established under a dictatorship and it has been controlled and directed by that dictatorship since its inception. It therefore cannot be said to represent the unfettered will of the people of Ghana. The MFJ certainly believes that a strong local government system is a necessary foundation for democratic government. This must, however, be fashioned by the people themselves in conditions of freedom and by their elected representatives, and not be decreed by a desperate and departing military regime.

Further, the NCD report and the PNDC's "constitutional proposals" on decentralization of administration seek, among others, to entrench the so-called "revolutionary organs" of the PNDC in the future constitution of Ghana (see NCD report, page 16). Though decentralized administration is an important feature of a viable democracy, this attempt to smuggle the PNDC's 'revolutionary organs' into the future constitution is illegitimate and must be rejected.

The attempt to entrench the "consolidation and directions of the (PNDC's) Economic Recovery Programme" in the constitution of the Fourth Republic is the hallmark of dictatorship and political arrogance. As a broad coalition of different political forces and social interests, the MFJ does not have any official position on the future economic policy of the country and therefore has no specific position on the ERP. But whatever economic policy will be pursued is a matter for Ghanaians to decide by assessing the manifestoes and programmes of competing parties and voting for whichever they adjudge can best serve their interests. If, on the other hand, there is the need for a "national consensus" on the direction of the economy it is best done by the genuine organized political forces, the parties, and not by a military regime whose rule is about to end. The attempt to determine in advance the future course of the economy by imposing the ERP on the constitution would amount to putting the future government in an economic strait-jacket.

The PNDC's decision to put its draft constitution before the people for adoption through a national referendum is not only cumbersome but also dubious. The constitution of a country is a composite document with many provisions, and to decree that Ghanaians vote a simple "yes" or "no" on such a document gives the people no real choice. What a great waste it would be if, after all the processes, the people voted against the constitution! In fact, the PNDC's policy is no more than an attempt to force through its constitution clothed in some democratic trapping but tailored to meet its needs as a departing military regime.

[ ] After a careful consideration of the PNDC's statement on the NCD report, and comparing it with the main demands of the people and their mood, the MFJ has come to the definite conclusion that the statement and the constitutional proposals contained in it fall far short of the basic demands of Ghanaians and their expectations. It must therefore be rejected *in toto* and we hereby reject the statement as a fraud on the people. The real aim of the government statement and the apparent concessions contained in it is to SIDE-STEP and CONTAIN the basic demands of the people and to DISARM the nation-wide movement for democracy from exerting greater pressure for the attainment of all its democratic demands. The PNDC hopes, by this means, to break the unity and determination of the people and seize the initiative so that it can proceed to impose its own constitution on the country.

The government statement has exposed the absolute bad faith of the PNDC and its determination to have its way irrespective of the will of Ghanaians. That is why Ghanaians of all walks of life are so incensed and angered by the statement. By failing to meet the basic demands of the people and proceeding to use state resources to organize its forces, the PNDC has shown conclusively that it has no moral right nor political legitimacy to continue to rule and to supervize the crucial stages left on the road to establishing a sound and viable democracy in Ghana. We therefore demand the IMMEDIATE RESIGNATION of the PNDC and the transfer of the power of government to a NATIONAL TRANSITIONAL GOVERNMENT headed by the Chief Justice, and made up of a representative of the PNDC and *bona fide* representatives of authentic public organizations. This, in our view, will facilitate a *speedy* and *peaceful* transition to democracy in Ghana.

From the platform of this press conference, the MFJ calls on all democratic forces in the country, all genuine and representative public organizations and all Ghanaians of goodwill to *unite* and *reject* this new act of dictatorship and political arrogance.

We call on all independent public organizations to take immediate steps to convene a genuine and representative *Constitutional Conference* to determine the processes by which our country shall be returned to constitutional and democratic rule.

[ ] At a press conference on 5 April, 1991, the MFJ called on the PNDC to meet the seven basic demands of the people "by the end of April . . . before any further steps are taken in the processes leading to democracy". We warned that if the PNDC refused to heed the demands and aspirations of the people for multi-party democracy, "the people will have no alternative but to vote for multi-party democracy with their feet in the streets". April has come to an end, and the PNDC has still not met any of the seven basic demands of the people. It has rather taken the final step towards imposing its constitutional programme on the country. It is obvious that the PNDC will not heed the demands of the people unless it is compelled to do so. We are therefore calling on all democratic forces, all the major public organizations, all honest and patriotic Ghanaians to unite and prepare to back the seven basic demands and the demand for the transfer of the powers of government to a transitional government with MASS AND PEACEFUL DEMONSTRATION.

> MFJ — FOURTH REPUBLIC!
> BOYCOTT THE CONSULTATIVE BODY!
> DOWN WITH DICTATORSHIP!
> MULTI-PARTY DEMOCRACY NOW!!!
> LONG LIVE GHANA!!!

Signed.
Johnny F. S. Hansen Akoto Ampaw
(1st Vice Chairman) *(Executie Member)*

John Ndebugre Obeng Manu
(National Organizer) *(National Secretary)*

A. Owusu Gyimah Dan Lartey
(Executive Member) *(National Treasurer)*

Dr. Dsane Selby Kwesi Pratt Jnr.
(National Executive Member) *(Deputy National Secretary)*

F. T. Darko Kwame Wiafe
(National Executive Member) *(National Executive Member)*

DOCUMENT 15

GHANA BAR ASSOCIATION

Statement on the Return to Constitutional Rule

The National Commission for Democracy has recently published its report on the outcome of the regional debates sponsored by it on the future constitutional structure of Ghana. Upon the submission of the report to the Provisional National Defence Council, the Chairman of the Provisional National Defence Council (PNDC) indicated that the method of selecting the membership of the "broad-based national consultative committee", which will deliberate on the report, will be announced by the end of May 1991 to permit the committee to begin its work in July 1991. The Ghana Bar Association (GBA), which has consistently and courageously championed the cause of constitutional government in our country, views with great concern the manner in which the programme for the restoration of constitutional government is unfolding.

Firstly, the business of making a constitution for the nation is a matter that concerns all citizens of this country. It cannot be done in an open and transparent manner if laws exist which hamper the citizen's freedom of expression, and which threaten his liberty. The Ghana Bar Association therefore calls upon the PNDC Government to demonstrate its sincerity to the process of fashioning a democratic future for the country to repeal immediately all repressive laws, namely PNDC Laws 4, 78, 91, 211 and 221 as a necessary condition for any meaningful deliberation on the country's future. Suspicions about a secret agenda of the PNDC will continue to flourish so long as the making of a new Constitution is conducted in a repressive and autocratic climate.

Secondly, the GBA views with great concern the concept of the "broad-based national consultative committee". As fashioned, this body would seem to have no teeth, but will be merely a consultative body to the PNDC. The only body capable of providing a Constitution for the nation is a Constituent Assembly, properly so-called. The GBA notes that the [the report on the] National Commission for Democracy [ ] speaks of a "Consultative Assembly". Such an assembly must have more than consultative functions — it must have the power to promulgate a new Constitution for the country. Without such a power, its deliberations will be ultimately meaningless, since at the end of the day the promulgating body will be the PNDC itself. This would be an unfortunate development for the future stability of the country. The PNDC should clarify immediately the functions and responsibilities of the Assembly in a manner that indicates clearly that it is this body, not the PNDC, which will enact the new Constitution.

Thirdly, the composition of the Constituent Assembly. The 1969 and 1979 Constitutions were the result of the deliberations of Constituent Assemblies whose members were selected by "identifiable groups". The GBA reiterates that the constituent Assembly should under no circumstances be hand-picked. The Ghana Bar Association believes that the formulae used on these occasions are well-suited to the present task, and calls upon the Government to give a clear indication to the country as to the basis of selection of the members of the Constituent Assembly.

Lastly, there is no doubt that little confidence will be engendered in the constitution-making process if it is supervised by a PNDC organ such as the NCD. Objectivity and impartiality are required of a body that supervises electoral processes. Only an independent, electoral body, which the NCD is not, can meet this requirement. The GBA is thus calling upon the PNDC Government to abolish forthwith the NCD, especially as it has completed its work, and replace it with a genuinely independent electoral commission.

Issued by the Ghana Bar Association on this 25 day of April, 1991.

Signed: A. K. Mmieh, Esq. SAC
             (National President)

             P. Adu-Gyamfi, Esq.
             (National Secretary)

DOCUMENT 16

Statement of the Ghana Bar Association Made at an Emergency General Meeting of the Bar on Saturday 11 May 1991 on the NCD Report and the PNDC's Statement on the Said Report

It will be recalled that at an Emergency General Meeting of the Ghana Bar Association (GBA) held in Accra on Saturday 23 February 1991, the GBA reacted to the Chairman of the PNDC's New Year Address to the Nation on the Programme for a Return to Constitutional Rule in Ghana, *inter alia*, as follows:

i) The PNDC should set out a clear timetable for a Return to Constitutional Rule in Ghana;

ii) Free and fair elections should be held to usher in a new Civilian Administration;

iii) There was an urgent need for the establishment of a Constituent Assembly with the power to promulgate a future Constitution for Ghana;

iv) The NCD which is an integral part of the PNDC should be abolished and an Independent Electoral Commission be established to organize and supervise the conduct of future elections in Ghana;

v) All repressive Laws, amongst which are PNDC Laws 4, 78, 91, 211 and 221 which bear upon the liberty and freedom of expression of citizens of Ghana be repealed;

vi) That all persons in political detention be released forthwith and that a general amnesty be granted to all Ghanaian exiles.

It will further be recalled that when on the presentation of the NCD Report to the PNDC on 20th March, 1991 the Chairman indicated that "a broad-based national Consultative Committee" would be elected to deliberate on the NCD Report. The GBA again by statement dated on the 25 April 1991 reiterated its stand on the matter by calling upon the PNDC Government to:

i) Repeal all repressive and draconian laws on the Statute books which hamper freedom of expression and undermine individual liberties;

ii) Establish a Constituent Assembly which has power to -deliberate on and promulgate the future Constitution for Ghana instead of the so-called "Consultative Assembly" which lacks the powers to promulgate the Constitution;

iii) Give a clear indication to the country as to the basis of selection of members to the Constituent Assembly bearing in mind our previous experiences in 1969 and 1979;

iv) Abolish the NCD and in its stead establish a genuinely Independent Electoral Commission.

After a careful study of the Report of the NCD on "The Establishment of a New Democratic Order", for Ghana and after a thorough analysis of the PNDC's statement on the said Report published on Friday 10 May 1991, the GBA hereby reiterates its views which touch on and concern Democratic Constitutional Rule in Ghana as contained in GBA's statements issued on 4 October 1990, 23 February 1991 and 25 April 1991 and further Resolves as follows:

1. The Drafting and Promulgation of a Constitution for Ghana should be the responsibility of a Constituent Assembly and not the so-called "Consultative Committee" as announced by the Government. The membership of the said Constituent Assembly should be elected based on Constituency Basis in a free, fair, open and direct elections conducted by an Independent Electoral Commission upon the principle of Universal Adult Suffrage and *funded by government*.

2. The GBA is of the view that Ghana is a predominately illiterate society: a complex document such as a "Constitution" cannot therefore be approved or rejected by the people by a Yes or No vote at a Referendum. The suggestion by the PNDC of a Referendum is designed to hoodwink Ghanaians and the GBA therefore calls upon the PEOPLE OF GHANA to reject such a suggestion.

3. In view of the fact that the members of the PNDC, "Revolutionary Organs", Cadres of the Revolution and The 31st December Women's Movement are openly engaged in political campaigns under the guise of duty tours and seminars, even though there is an official ban on politics, the GBA calls upon the PNDC to officially lift the ban on political activities forthwith so as to ensure free expression of contrary views by all Ghanaians which is the hallmark of true Democracy.

4. It has come to the notice of the GBA that PNDC has instructed tha views of certain groups and individuals should never be reported or printed by the government-controlled print and electronic media. Since fair and democratic elections cannot be conducted where opposing views are suppressed, the GBA calls upon the PNDC to remove forthwith all such restrictions to make accessible to all and

sundry the use of the print and electronic media so as to create a congenial atmosphere for a peaceful transition to Constitutional Rule in Ghana. In furtherance of this objective the GBA calls upon the Government to repeal, as a matter of urgency, all repressive laws in our Statute Books which hamper and restrict Human and People's Rights, among which are PNDC Laws 4, 78, 91, 211 and 221.

5. At page 18 of the NCD Report, members of the NCD, quite rightly in our view, recognized the need for a "neutral NCD in the new Constitutional Order". This recognition is an honest admission by members of the NCD that the NCD is not "Neutral" but an integral part of PNDC's political machinery. The GBA calls upon the PNDC to abolish the NCD forthwith and set up an Independent Electoral Commission . . .

6. The GBA mindful of the need that the process of return to Constitutional Rule should be done in an atmosphere of peace and tranquility: realizing that it is imperative that all Ghanaians have an inalienable right and indeed an obligation to be involved in the said process: being aware that Ghanaians who would make substantial contributions to the process of change are in forced exile, calls upon the PNDC to declare an Unconditional Amnesty to all political exiles and release all those who have been convicted of political offences and those in detention without trial, so that all Ghanaians may be involved in the process of Constitution-making.

7. Bearing in mind the fact that the people of Ghana have overwhelmingly opted for a Multi-Party political system, the GBA is of the view that all National, Regional, District and Local elections ought to be conducted under Party Political Basis.

8. Finally, in order to ensure a smooth and peaceful transition to Constitutional Rule in Ghana, the GBA calls upon the PNDC to hand over the administration of government by 1 July 1991 to a Neutral Interim Administration whose duty would be to usher in the 4th Republic by 1 July 1992. The GBA suggests that the composition of the Interim Administration be made up as follows:

a) The Chief Justice of Ghana —*Chairman*
b) The President, National House of Chiefs — *Member*
c) A Representative of the Christian Council of Ghana — *Member*
d) A Representative of the National Catholic Secretariat — *Member*
e) A Representative of the Moslem Council — *Member*
f) A Representative of Ghana National Association of Teachers — *Member*
g) A Representative of the Association of Recognized Professional

Bodies — *Member*
h) A Representative of Revolutionary Organs — *Member*
i) A Representative of the Trades Union Congress — *Member*
j) A Representative of National Union of Farmers and Fishermen — *Member*
k) A Representative of National Council on Women and Development— *Member*
l) A Representative of the National Union of Ghana Students — *Member*

Dated at Accra, this 13 day of May, 1991.

(Sgd.)
Paul Adu-Gyamfi
(National Secretary)
Ghana Bar Association

Anthony K. Mmieh
(National President)
Ghana Bar Association

DOCUMENT 17

Memorandum from the Heads of the Member Churches of the Christian Council of Ghana and the Catholic Bishops' Conference on the Release of the Report on the Evolving Democratic Process

We, the Heads of Churches of the Christian Council and the Catholic Bishops' Conference of Ghana note with gratitude the steps the Provisional National Defence Council (PNDC) Government has taken resulting in the publication of the Report by the National Commission on Democracy on the emerging democratic process in the country, in which process our two bodies have actively participated.

We have also noted the pronouncements of the Head of State on the receipt of the Report and we are pleased that this has been published and made available to the public.

We had hoped, however, that the Government would issue a White Paper alongside the Report setting out its position on the Report as has been the custom in the past. This has not been done. We would humbly urge that it be done without delay.

This White Paper would provide a clear and definitive time-table, spelling out the steps that would be followed and when each stage would be implemented. It would also give a clear indication as to how representation to the various bodies in the process would be elected. These bodies should be technically competent and representative of the various shades of opinion in the country.

The White Paper should repeat the known traditional practice in the past in which identifiable national groupings such as the Ghana Bar Association, the Ghana National Association of Teachers, the Christian Council of Ghana, The National Catholic Secretariat, Council on Women and Development, the National House of Chiefs etc., as well as others which may have subsequently emerged would have representatives.

In view of the above, we respectfully request the PNDC Government to:
1. publish the Government White Paper on the Report as soon as possible;
2. take steps towards the setting up of an independent electoral body which would supervise all elections in the process, and which would

have adequate resources to do its work effectively;
3. lift the ban on political parties as soon as possible to enable the people to organize themselves openly for the elections;
4. take the necessary steps to implement the following which we believe would generate the right atmosphere for a healthy political activity in the country;
   a) repeal certain laws in the country, especially PNDCL 4, PNDCL 91, PNDCL 221, and the relevant sections of PNDCL 78 which deals with executions for political offences;
   b) release all political prisoners and detainees;
   c) grant an unconditional amnesty for all political exiles.

We pray that the Almighty God will continue to guide and direct the PNDC Government and to give its members the courage, the determination, and the will to carry through the noble exercise they have begun in the interest of the people of Ghana and to the Glory of the Living God.

May the Lord be with you.

(Sgd.)
Rt. Rev. Peter K. Sarpong
President of the Bishops' Conference

Rev. Fr. A. D. Balee
Secretary General, National Catholic Secretariat

Rt. Rev. Prof. K. A. Dickson
Chairman, Christian Council of Ghana

Rev. D.A. Dartey
General Secretary, Christian Council of Ghana

DOCUMENT 18

The Inaugural Address on the Occasion of the First Session of the Consultative Assembly by Flt.-Lt. J. J. Rawlings, Chairman of the P.N.D.C. and Head of State, 26 August 1991

[ ] We have gathered here today to initiate yet another step forward in the process which we began almost ten years ago of building new democratic institutions which are responsive to the aspirations of our people and are organic consequences of our social, historical, economic and political experiences.

I wish on behalf of the PNDC and on my own behalf to congratulate you Mr. Speaker, and the Honourable Members of the National Consultative Assembly and its officers. Whether elected or appointed, your presence here is testimony of your commitment to our nation's future.

[ ] Your duty and responsibility is heavy. But I wish to remind you that the responsibility is not to the P.N.D.C. It is not even primarily to the people of your district or organization who have sent you here, in so far as their group interests may be concerned. Your responsibility is first and foremost to all Ghanaian citizens of this country, to the present and future generations, and your overriding criterion for deciding upon any constitutional provision must be whether it will enhance the well-being, peace and unity of our whole nation.

I also wish to commend the Committee of Experts, whose intellectual labours within a very limited time-frame, have given us a worthy basic document for the deliberations of this Assembly.

We should also all give thanks to all those whose efforts have in diverse ways contributed to the attainment of the stage we have now reached. This includes those whose criticisms whether positive or not, have led to a synthesis of ideas relevant to our democratic future.

[ ] The last decade of the twentieth century will certainly be remembered as one of the most spectacular and eventful of transitional times. We have seen the growth of *detente* between the seemingly rigid power blocs of East and West. We have seen the reunification of Germany. And we are witnesses to the changes taking place in the Soviet Union.

In many countries on our own continent, various political and administrative structures are facing their first challenges in decades. These challenges are characterized by manifestations of mass discontent and dissatisfaction with systems which had long failed to provide their people access to the decision-making process.

We in Ghana experienced our share of such crises and went through the worst of them from the mid-seventies through 4 June 1979 and up to the trying years of 1982 and 1983. Indeed, we still have our challenges, but these are in a large measure the product of not only our economic achievements but also of the development of a new political consciousness borne out by the revolt.

Today, after all the toil and sacrifices, we are in a position to point to certain positive achievements which have been recorded under the socio-economic transformation that has been taking place over the past nine and half years. We have witnessed Ghana's recovery of the place which our proud nation used to have in the community of nations, and we have witnessed our people's recovery of confidence and pride.

As a people, we must assimilate the lessons of the past, which should guide us so as to avoid making the same mistakes again. In this respect it is crucial that we consolidate and sustain our modest economic achievements and reflect in our future constitution a concern to maintain the momentum of economic growth without of course, constraining the capacity of a government to respond effectively to the ever-changing circumstances of our globally-related national economy.

[ ] Our political agenda, which has been pursued in conjunction with the Economic Recovery Programme, has derived from major lessons learned during the June 4 period and its aftermath. The events of that period clearly demonstrated that whilst injustices could eventually arouse the ferocious anger of ordinary Ghanaians, that anger could not be transformed into sustainable and constructive action without the creation of relevant structures or institutions, together with the provision of opportunities for ordinary men and women to experience the practical realities of making and monitoring decisions in order to rediscover the sense of confidence, responsibility and competence which had been eroded by decades of political marginalization.

I believe that we now have a generation of men and women who know through practical experience that government involves much more than periodically casting a vote. By their involvement in Unit Committees, Town and Area Councils, in the District Assemblies, in the work-place CDRs, on the panels of Tribunals at various levels, and in the Mobisquads, thousands of people who previously would have been passive onlookers are now familiar with the practical issues of planning, budgeting, revenue collection, initiating and monitoring projects and programmes and the many practical details which go into the functioning of our society at

the Community, local and district level.

In other words, "Government" is no longer a remote and shadowy entity located in the regional capital but the everyday business of taking and monitoring decisions which affect us in our homes and communities. With the experience of nine and half years behind us, I believe that the people of this country are more ready than ever [for] *(sic)* this exercise of fashioning a constitution.

[ ] The achievements we have so far recorded have been made within the framework of structures which, as I have often emphasized, are provisional. The exercise which you begin today therefore represents the final stages of the processes which are phasing out the provisional structures, in order to ensure the continuity of the advances which have been made, and certainly not to return to the previous situation.

Any objective observer who has watched or participated in events in this country over the past nine and half years will have witnessed a consistent pattern, a sequence moving towards the establishment of a just and lasting democratic system embodying the will of the people. This Consultative Assembly is the next logical step in this process which began on 31 December, 1981.

[ ] We have faith in the people of Ghana, in the humblest citizen of our land and I have emphasized the need to root this Constitution in the people, in their hears *(sic)* and minds. So often in the past, constitutions have seemed mysterious and far away from the majority of our people; they have appeared to be the mysterious preserve of learned men who are isolated from the ordinary folk.

Because of this, I have to admit that some ordinary people have expressed some anxiety about our programme to establish a new constitution. Are we just returning to the old times, they ask. Are we returning to those times when the selected few determined the destiny of all of us? The people of this nation have no wish to return to the conditions which ignited their anger in 1979 and 1981.

I would like to assure the country that for us in the PNDC this is not a return to some previous order that was far removed from the ordinary man. This is still the people's time because it is a time of democracy, a time to give further institutional shape to the democratic stirring in our hearts which led to 4 June as well as 31 December. This is what constitutions have really meant in the history of humanity and the world.

The French Constitution, the Soviet Constitution, the American Constitution all came about from revolutions that overthrew previous orders in which ordinary people had been marginalized. The Constitutions gave clear and institutionalized expression to the power of the people to the new democracy that was being established in preference to the preceding orders.

Our constitution-making process arises out of our own circumstances of struggle just as theirs did. History shows that whilst the anger of the masses can overturn old structures of injustice, the energy of the masses needs to be channelled within new and relevant institutions and social structures in order to guarantee progress in the future.

In affirming our faith in the people, however humble their profession, however simple their background, we believe that it is ordinary people, in farms, in the factories, in the schools and universities, in the barracks, in the markets, in the streets, who, once they identify themselves with a cause, are prepared to defend it even at the cost of their lives.

We saw this on 19 June 1993 when ordinary Ghanaians, including many unarmed civilians refused to accept the presumption of a few misguided elements who thought they could take power away from the people and negate the progress that we had slowly begun to make. And so we have the experience of people defending what they cherish.

[ ] As a Government we are more interested in a constitution which provides for and guarantees freedom, justice, peace and stability for our people as opposed to some constitutions that seek to provide for the peace and stability of a government.

[ ] Unless this constitution is somehow different in character from those which have gone before, and unless it manages to capture some of the imponderables which make such a document unique to the people, we run the danger of finding ourselves back to where we began.

A constitution is only alive if it is borne up by probity and accountability. Probity and accountability are only alive if they are borne up by truth and integrity. Truth and integrity can only become a weapon to defend the honour and well-being of a nation when that weapon is held by both the rulers and the ruled. In the hands of only one of them, it becomes a dagger turned against those who hold it. No human society can progress in a creatively cohesive path without establishing the most basic line of integrity.

[ ] Integrity cannot be translated into words on paper. It is necessary to have checks and balances as well as penalties for lack of integrity.

The most basic of the foundations for a good constitution in human society are a commitment to truth and to integrity in human relationships. Where truth itself is no longer valued, where the sense of truth-telling as a virtue is no longer a firm baseline for social conduct, then the very fabric of society is in jeopardy, constitution or no constitution! Especially from those into whose hands society entrusts certain responsibilities, we must expect adherence to this baseline, otherwise the trust which simple men and women of integrity repose in their leaders, the faith of ordinary people in those who rule over them, can soon turn into a noose around our peoples' necks.

The missing ingredient, [ ] therefore, has been how to exact probity and accountability in our utterances and actions. Without this ingredient, we may have a document which provides for every possible contingency, and yet for the lack of this vital ingredient it will be a dead piece of paper, and also lack the capacity to inspire and kindle our nation's spirit.

[ ] Our purpose of a constitution is to lay down a legal framework for the governance of a nation. What we call the "Rule of Law" lays down procedures which must be followed in the case of any eventuality. This is meant to safeguard the interests of the disadvantaged and the voiceless, on the sad assumption that those who hold authority will tend to abuse it unless constrained by the Rule of Law.

All too often, however, the Rule of Law becomes a double-edged sword which works to the disadvantage of the majority. Our people become lost in its procedural delays and complexities. How can we therefore evolve a Rule of Law which avoids the stifling of initiative and has the flexibility to react to obvious and immediate injustices?

Otherwise the Rule of Law, as we all know from many experiences, becomes a straight jacket which condemns humble oppressed people to choose between long years of complex and expensive procedures, or a fatalistic acceptance of their lot. What is required now is a constitution that is revolutionary in nature. This is what our people have fought for. It is for you to create an atmosphere that gives meaning to the people's notion of fairness and justice as opposed to the atmosphere created by the constraint of the Rule of Law.

[ ] It is the view of the PNDC that a constitution need not be an excessively detailed and cumbersome document. Where this is so, the important principles tend to be obscured by the mass of detail, so that the ordinary citizen loses sight of the essence of the constitution and comes to regard it simply as a source of political quibbles and point-scoring.

Some of the most durable constitutions in the world are brief and simple, laying down the guiding principles which reflect the hopes and aspirations of their people, as well as setting out the relationships and the checks and balances between the various organs of State. However, I would wish you to give very special attention to certain areas.

[ ] The women of Ghana constitute a majority of our population. Their dynamism in our socio-economic life, their key role in ensuring domestic stability and prosperity, indeed their role in the production of life itself, makes it inexcusable and undemocratic for anyone to try to marginalize them in our nation's affairs. The need for constitutional

recognition of this issue has been highlighted in the Report of the Committee of Experts; previous to that the work of the Law Reform Commission provided the basis for the Government of the PNDC to express its democratic commitments by enacting a number of laws that sought to protect women and ensure respect for them in all social circumstances. I sincerely hope that this Consultative Assembly will deliberate on further measures that will give women in Ghana equality of opportunity and equal participation in the social and political decision-making.

Related to this and of special importance are the right of children to responsible parenthood. I wish to stress the right of children for responsible parenthood because it is a self-generating value which helps provide responsible citizens.

Ladies and gentlemen, you have before you among other basic documents, the Report of the Committee of Constitutional Experts. Before it was made available to the public, there were attempts in some quarters to describe this document as a PNDC-dictated draft Constitution.

It should be clear by now that this is not the case. Whilst we provided certain guide-posts, it is also the reaction of a panel of independent-minded constitutional experts to the varied opinions expressed by members of the public in the regional fora, and informed, by our previous constitutional experiences as well as their own expertise and knowledge of what is workable.

It is a sound working document within the given framework, reflecting what are, in the opinion of the Committee of Experts, the predominant issues confronting our nation.

You will also have noted, in your study of the Report, that no conclusive recommendation have been made in some areas, for example the representation of the people. It sets out various alternatives, with their advantages and disadvantages, to assist you in arriving at the most appropriate decisions. But even where the Committee of Experts makes a firm recommendation, you are free to amend, to add or subtract, as your reason and conscience may suggest after the consideration.

In this task, the Committee of Experts is at your disposal, to explain technicalities, to provide you with more examples from our past constitutions and from other countries as well as to assist you in transforming ideas into workable legal terms.

It is expected that each one of you will maintain close liaison with the organizations and Districts which you represent, explaining the issues under discussion and reflecting the views of your commitments in this Assembly.

As you know [ ] in our traditions in Ghana, consultations and consultative processes are at the heart of governing. The chief as you know, is supposed to consult regularly with his elders, the leaders are supposed to consult regularly with the community, sometimes formally, or other times informally. Those who rule are required to remember that they exercise a trust on behalf of the whole community and that their conduct is subject to the judgement of the people. The Government of the PNDC has been very concerned to follow these traditions that are so deep-rooted in our way of life.

However, I am told that you will have a recess during the period of the Non-Aligned Ministerial Conference. This will provide you with an opportunity to have some detailed consultations with your constituents.

[ ] The Committee of Experts has included in its Report certain matters which normally, if we were to follow the precedent of previous Assemblies of this kind, would have been legislated for by the government in office prior to the promulgation of a new constitution. These include matters relating to the representation of the people, local government, and the modalities for the registration and conduct of political formations and organisations. The Report also deals with the independence of the mass media. We therefore await the benefit of the collective wisdom of this Assembly on these issues, and the verdict of the people in the Referendum.

In this way you would have addressed not only the general framework of the constitutional order but also some of the mechanisms required for bringing into effect the elements of the new order. In effect this is a unique opportunity for you as representatives of the people to deliberate and make recommendations on a wider range of issues.

This Assembly will also have to make a recommendation on one of the options given by the Committee of Experts on the body or institution which will conduct future elections. For obvious reasons, this issue must be settled before the Referendum.

[ ] On the assumption that you will complete your work within the estimated time-frame, the Referendum will be held in January or at the latest February 1992 which will enable the people of this country decide whether to give their seal of approval to your efforts. The referendum will also constitute our individual and collective oath of allegiance to the Constitution and a commitment to defend its principles.

Within two weeks of the outcome of the Referendum, appropriate legislation will be enacted on those issues which require it, such as representation of the people, and political organizations.

[ ] This Assembly must conduct itself in a non-partisan atmosphere. I therefore wish to restate that there will be no lifting of the ban on partisan political activities whilst this Consultative Assembly is engaged in its

important task. To do so would be an insult to the Members of this Assembly, who must first debate the rules for the conduct of political activities and the formation of political organisations.

[ ] With the mandate of the people and under the new constitution, and allowing for the necessary legislative processes, the Presidential and Parliamentary elections will be held at the latest by the last quarter of 1992.

I should also inform this Assembly that international observers will be invited to witness both the Referendum and the Presidential and Parliamentary elections.

[ ] Our nation looks to you to carry out your duties with dedication, objectivity and commitment, without fear or favour. Whilst you should not lobby for parochial or divisive interests, you should safeguard with all your might the interests of the disadvantaged in our society. Whilst you should strive to allow room for the rich diversity of our nation, you should also strive to emphasize those factors which bring about national unity.

To those of you who, as Members of this Consultative Assembly, have been given the privilege and grave responsibility of deliberating on behalf of the people of this country, I wish to say that you carry in your hands, like an egg, the hopes of all Ghanaians. The quality of your dedication, objectivity and faithfulness to the aspirations of those for whom you speak will determine whether this egg will be broken, or if it hatches, whether it will bring forth a vulture or a proud eagle.

I hope that, in saying this, I am not giving any comfort to members of some so-called "Eagle Club"! Ghana's Eagle which features on our national crest and which was used so eloquently by Dr. Aggrey of blessed memory to exemplify our proud national potential is not the prerogative of any group of individuals.

[ ] Our actions and the decisions we take today must stand the test of time. May it be said that this Assembly gave to the people of Ghana a living constitution. And may it be said that the totality of our efforts as a people made it possible.

[ ] I commend to you the Report of the Committee of Constitutional Experts as a basic working paper for the general guidance of this gathering in their onerous task.

Chiana Pe Rowland Ayagitam, your abilities and statesmanship are not unknown. I commit this Assembly into your hands. May you guide its deliberations well and may God bless your endeavours. [ ]

Section Three
1992/(1993)

Introduction

The preceding year had been equally momentous. A Consultative Assembly had been inaugurated to write a new constitution for the new republic that was in the making. Before then the PNDC government's refusal to negotiate the transition process with the pro-democracy forces as well as its tight control over the political process, especially its refusal to repeal what the pro-democracy forces regarded as "draconian" or "oppressive" laws and lift the ban on party politics, had decisively limited various forms of political expression.

The pro-democracy forces responded by developing alternative strategies of political struggle to force the PNDC to open up the political arena to other contenders for power: they formed several seemingly non-political civic associations. Among such associations were The Danquah-Busia Memorial Club, Great Unity Club, Our Heritage, Kwame Nkrumah Welfare Society, Kwame Nkrumah Youngsters Club, and the Ex-CPP Group. As these associations were formed, the general public was left in no doubt that they were intended as dummies for future political parties. In particular the public statements of those civic associations betrayed their hidden intentions and true political identities — either as loyalist of the Danquah-Busia political tradition or the Nkrumah political tradition. They, together with others, later formed the Coordinating Committee of Democratic Forces.

In response to this open challenge from the pro-democracy forces, the pro-Rawlings, Pro-PNDC supporters, who were concentrated in the various grassroots organizations, also formed their own dummy associations — for example, the Eagle Club, Friends of the Progressive Decade, Rawlings Fan Club, New Nation Club, Development Union, and the Development Club. In due course they also came together under one umbrella organization, the United Clubs for Rawlings. However it had become clear that the PNDC's resistance to political reforms was crumbling under the pressure for multi-party politics. But it was equally clear that the PNDC gorvenment was also preparing, however reluctantly, to engage in multi-party politics. Indeed even those who did not believe in democracy were becoming reluctant converts to democratic politics. Even in the Consultative Assembly the shadows of the future multi-party politics and democratic political discourse were powerfully evident as groups and factions formed around old and new political traditions at the same time as they cooperated to fashion a new democratic constitution for the people of Ghana.

The major event that finally gave impetus to these shadows of democratic politics was the referendum of 28 April 1992. On that day the people of Ghana gave massive approval to what has come to be known as *The 1992 Constitution*.

Another crucial development added substance to the sinews of democratic politics. This was the emergence of the *private press* which provided necessary scaffolding to strengthen the emerging political structure for democracy. Within a short space of time various privately owned newspapers had hit the news stand. This was a veritable revolution in the sense that the (re) emergence of private newspapers like the *Free Press, Ghanaian Voice, Ghanaian Chronicle, The Guide, The Independent* and others effectively broke the government's monopoly over the dissemination of information. But the private press did not just become an alternative voice for the pro-democracy forces. More especially they greatly facilitated the further expansion of the political space for democratic politics. Their role in ensuring that 1992 would pass with the death of the military regime is indeed immortal.

From 18 May 1992 when the ban on party politics was lifted the vast majority of the civic associations that had engaged the military government in that relentless struggle for liberty were absorbed into the political parties that had formed. The following political parties did announce their presence:

Democratic Peoples Party
New Generation Party
Ghana Democratic Republican Party
National Independence Party
Peoples Heritage Party
Egle Party
National Convention Party
National Democratic Congress
New Patriotic Party
People's National Convention
People's Party for Democracy and Development
National Justice Party, and
National Salvation Party

Some of these' could not survive long enough to either witness, or participate in, the presidential and parliamentary elections of November-December 1992.

As usual the parties which survived became preoccupied with winning political power and much less concerned than before with liberalizing the military regime. As the energies of the new political parties were channelled into the struggle for state power, the Ghana

Bar Association, the NUGS, the GTUC, the Christian Council of Ghana and the Catholic Bishops Conference remained steadfast crusaders in the fight to democratize the politics and government of the country. Among these, the Ghana Bar Association and especially the private press were the most vociferous, militant and consistent.

DOCUMENT 19

NUGS Statement on the PNDC's Time Table on the Return to Constitutional Rule

The National Union of Ghana Students (NUGS) has been abreast with the on-going *(sic)* in the political scene and wishes to express its views on the PNDC's Time-Table for the return to Constitutional Rule.

We wish to state emphatically that the Chairman of the PNDC woefully failed in his speech on the 5 March, 1992, to address very crucial issues like;

    (i) Repealing of the repressive laws; PNDC Law 4, PNDC Law 78, PNDC Law 91, etc.

    (ii) Granting of unconditional amnesty to political exiles.

    (iii) The immediate release of all political prisoners languishing in condemned cells.

These issues represent the genuine demands of the Ghanaian citizenry and it is unfortunate that any political time table in a time of transition and reconciliation should lose sight of the people's demands.

The NUGS reiterates that to ensure a peaceful transition to Constitutional Rule, the PNDC must hand over to an Interim Government headed by the Chief Justice by the end of March, 1992. This will ensure that dubious provisions are not inserted into the constitution as in the case of 1979.

The intransigence on the referendum on the draft constitution is not only a duplication of efforts and funds but completely irrelevant. It is in view of such absurdity that we initially called for a Constituent Assembly of equal representation of recognized bodies which could promulgate a constitution for the nation. It is not too late to amend the law enacting the Consultative Assembly to give it the power to promulgate the constitution to save Ghanaians the unnecessary trouble of a referendum that is highly questionable.

The NUGS condemns the existence of the National Commission for Democracy (NCD) after the establishment of an Independent Electoral Commission. The new electoral commission can adequately address the issue of political education and still conduct elections. That makes the continuous presence of the NCD redundant and unacceptable.

The unorthodox approach that has been adopted in making the

presidential elections precede parliamentary elections is very disturbing. Equally disturbing is the silence over the role of the armed revolutionary organs in this transitional period. We would like to know what role the PNDC has assigned them.

The sudden interruption of the academic programme at GIMPA by an emergency meeting of PNDC appointees is one of the many totalitarian manouvres of the Government. We are strongly of the view that this meeting which is being held behind closed doors at a time when there is a total ban on party politicking in Ghana is a stab in the back of Ghanaians. This is because we believe the aim of the meeting is to adopt campaign strategies to their advantage.

We would finally like to remind the self-appointed High Priests of probity and accountability that it is high time they show *(sic)* practical faith and commitment to their slogan. It is our expectation that they would subject themselves to this principle of probity and accountability for once. Any attempt to side-step this principle will be sheer hypocrisy at its best.

Issued by the National Executive Committee of NUGS on behalf of the entire student politic of Ghana.

Signed
John Samwin Banienuba
(National Secretary)

DOCUMENT 20

Statement by the Ghana Bar Association on the Transitional Provisions of the Constitution

It is essential to any constitution-making process that provision is made for the orderly transfer and succession of power and authority, especially after a period of ten years of military rule. This is the purpose of transitional provisions, and as the term connotes, such provisions should be transitional in nature and not have any permanent features or characteristics. It is for this reason that the Ghana Bar Association considers it a duty to warn the people of this country against the danger of putting into the constitution, which is coming out, transitional provisions similar to those inserted into the 1979 Constitution by the Armed Forces Revolutionary Council.

These provisions sought to perpetuate all acts and deeds of the Armed Forces Revolutionary Council and to give a blanket immunity to members of the Armed Forces Revolutionary Council, its agents or those purporting to act in its name. The effect of this was to prevent cases of manifest injustice and violations of human rights from being investigated and dealt with according to law. The spate of constitutional litigation that resulted from this contributed in no small measure to the downfall of the Third Republic. Such a situation must be avoided at all costs in the establishment of the Fourth Republic.

It is unthinkable that after ten years in which probity and accountability have been preached to this nation with unprecedented passion that those who preached this should attempt via the transitional provisions to escape the test which they themselves have laid down and enforced with sanguinary fervour. It would mean that the principles of probity and accountability were in fact a hoax, and may be compromised to suit the convenience of those who seized power and ruled this country by force of arms.

The principles of probity and accountability must be applied without exception to all those who wield power in this country. It is manifest hypocrisy and humbug for the people of this country to be told of the need to avoid corrupt and self-seeking "politicians" in civilian administrations if the same yardstick is not going to be applied to politicians in military garb.

It may well be necessary to grant coup-makers immunity from legal process for the act of staging the coup and overthrowing the constitution, an act which in ordinary circumstances constitutes the highest crime known to the criminal law, treason. Expediency, however, may render it necessary to provide such immunity especially after such a long interval of time. Beyond this there is no justification for granting any other form of immunity.

The Ghana Bar Association is as interested as all well-meaning Ghanaians in promoting peace and national reconciliation. The end, however, will be defeated by provisions that seek to condone gross violations of human rights, and outright criminal acts committed not only by the PNDC itself, but also by all the numerous appointees, who have in some cases taken the law into their hands and enriched themselves at the expense of the nation. The Fourth Republic will be built on very shaky foundations if probity and accountability are given such short shrift.

It is a pity that the publicity given to the constitutional proposals of the Asante Committee has not been extended to the proposals for the transitional provisions, which remain at this date still a closely guarded secret. The public interest requires that a full public debate and information on the proposals for the transitional provision should have preceded the adoption by the Consultative Assembly of such proposals.

It would set a dangerous precedent to insert into our new constitution provisions which authorize "appointees" of the PNDC to refuse to accept legal process whether in the form of writs or otherwise merely on the ground that the subject-matter of these processes are covered or alleged to be covered by a blanket provision of immunity granted to such "appointees" for all things whatsoever done or omitted to be done by them during the administration of the PNDC, for this would encourage and engender disrespect for the Constitution, the rule of law and legal processes generally by those who consider themselves to have been appointed by the PNDC and to have done or omitted to have done things alleged against them during the long administration of the PNDC.

Never in our constitutional history has such a provision been adopted or even contemplated. It should be obvious to all that until a writ or other legal process has been accepted and read, the person to whom it is intended or directed can never tell its subject-matter, let alone determine whether this relates to a particular type of appointee and a particular period in his life. Nothing should be done to let anyone think that he can treat the law and its processes with contempt because that way lies chaos and national disaster.

The Ghana Bar Association would like to appeal to the members of the Consultative Assembly to reject any proposals similar to those of the 1979 Constitution, which seek to perpetuate all acts and deeds of the PNDC, and grant a blanket immunity to its members and appointees. Dated at the National Secretariat, Accra, this 26th day of March 1992.

Signed
A.E. Mmieh, SAC　　　　　Paul Adu-Gyamfi Esq
National President　　　　*National Secretary.*

DOCUMENT 21

Statement by the Ghana Bar Association on the PNDC's Transitional Programme

The broadcast of 5 March 1992 by the Chairman of the PNDC, Flt.-Lt. Rawlings, in which he outlined his government's transitional programme for the restoration of democratic rule, welcome though that programme may be in principle, contains several unsatisfactory elements. As has been its wont, the Ghana Bar Association, which has in the last decade staunchly championed the cause of democracy and freedom in Ghana, despite officially-orchestrated abuses, threats and harassment of its leaders, conceives it to be the national duty to highlight the defects in the programme, so that public opinion can be peacefully mobilized for a more satisfactory programme.

It is our firm belief that the Referendum scheduled for 28th April 1992 is unnecessary and a waste of public funds. As a means of promulgating a Constitution, the referendum is wholly inappropriate, for it cannot provide an accurate reflection of people's attitudes. There can be no meaningful endorsement of a document as complex as a constitution by the referendum process. It appears to be merely a public relations exercise, which will be wasteful of scarce public resources. What indeed will be the issue formulated for the Referendum?

It is the view of the Ghana Bar Association that the Consultative Assembly, despite the initial misgivings of the Association, should be given the power to promulgate the Constitution. This will be a more satisfactory, and less wasteful method of bringing the Constitution into being. The Ghana Bar Association is therefore calling on the PNDC government to abandon the idea of the Referendum, and give the Consultative Assembly the power to promulgate the Constitution.

It is imperative that the correct atmosphere of peace, freedom, and reconciliation prevails during the transitional period. That cannot be achieved when certain repressive laws still disfigure our statute books, for the existence of such laws will seriously hinder the free exchange and expression of ideas which are central to a democratic process. The Ghana Bar Association is therefore reiterating its call for the PNDC to repeal forthwith all the repressive laws, such as PNDC Laws 4, 70 and 91 so that the political and constitutional debate can be conducted in a climate devoid of intimidation and fear. The Ghana Bar Association is of the view that this repeal should take place at the latest by the date of the publication of the proposals of the Consultative Assembly.

In the same vein, the conditional amnesty granted by the PNDC for the exiles should be transformed into an unconditional amnesty so that the nation will benefit from the contribution of all its children. Political prisoners, and persons being held for politically-related offences, should also be released forthwith to promote the process of national reconciliation.

The lifting of the ban on party political activity should not await 18 May 1992, for with the publication of the proposals of the Consultative Assembly there can be no further warrant for the ban. On the contrary, it will be important to allow the various political groups in the country the opportunity to mobilize public opinion for the constitutional exercise. The Ghana Bar Association is therefore calling on the PNDC to lift the ban on party political activity with the publication of the proposals of the Consultative Assembly.

Another serious defect in the PNDC's transitional programme is the staggering of the presidential and parliamentary elections. This is another unnecessary waste of public resources. These elections should, as the satisfactory example of 1979 provides, be held simultaneously. Whatever advantage is anticipated by the PNDC from the differentiation of the presidential and parliamentary elections is not in the public interest. The 1979 example should be followed. It is cheaper, and as 1979 proved, effectively understood by the broad masses of our people.

It is pertinent to point out that the fixing of dates for elections has historically been the function of the Electoral Commission, and that the fixing of the dates by the PNDC constitutes an unwarranted usurpation of the power and functions of the Interim Electoral Commission, a development that is disquieting for the future. The Ghana Bar Association is therefore calling upon the Interim Electoral Commission to exert its proper role, and insist that the presidential and parliamentary elections be held simultaneously. The Commission should resist any further encroachment on its prerogatives.

The Ghana Bar Association is of the view that all the processes for the restoration of democratic government can and must be completed this year. There would be no need, after eleven years of military rule, for there to be any further delays in the hand-over of power to a democratically elected government. It is essential that these processes be completed this year, so that the nation can begin its new life from the beginning of the next year. The new democratic government should be in place by 31 December 1992.

There are other aspects of the programme which call for comment.

It is now evident that some members and functionaries of the PNDC regime are interested in the competitive politics of the Fourth Republic. If so, candour with the people and fairness demand that such functionaries declare their intentions openly. The present, unedifying spectacle of rumour and suspicion does not advance the national interest. Those members and functionaries of the military regime who have political ambitions should have the courage of their convictions, declare their ambition and in the interest of fairness resign their office so that they can compete on the same basis as everyone else. There will then be no suspicion that public funds are being used to promote the personal, political campaign of members of the present government.

The broadcast of 5 March 1992 indicated that the rules governing the operations and activities of the political parties will be enacted after the Referendum. Since the PNDC regrettably acts unilaterally on all matters concerning the transition, it is essential that it recognizes the deep revulsion of the people of Ghana for any rules that may be patently undemocratic.

There should be no limitation of parties, there should be no disqualification provisions; and there should be no restrictions on party names and symbols. Our people are capable of deciding whom they wish to follow without having conditions imposed on them by an unelected and unrepresentative body, such as the PNDC.

Once again, the Ghana Bar Association is calling upon the PNDC to disband forthwith the so-called revolutionary organs, such as the CDRs, CDOs, the militia, 31st December Women's Movement, which are all financed out of public funds, and which serve as the political organs of the PNDC. Many of them also act as instruments of terror and harassment of innocent citizens, which thereby pose a threat to the peaceful and free exercise of the political rights of citizens of this country. They have no place in a democratic order, for the only bodies that should operate in a democracy are voluntary bodies, and not state-sponsored organs of political control.

The Ghana Bar Association is calling on the PNDC to ensure that by the date the ban on party political activities is lifted these organs will have been dismantled. It will be a sure way of promoting national reconciliation and unity.

Finally, the Ghana Bar Association wishes to caution the Consultative Assembly and the PNDC against any insertion into the Constitution the kind of Transitional Provisions which disfigured the 1979 Constitution. The whole concept of probity and accountability which the AFRC preached with bloody zeal and which the PNDC has continued to preach will be undermined and rendered meaningless if

members of the PNDC and their appointees are considered above the same concept.
Dated at the National Secretariat, Accra, this 20th day of March 1992.

(Sgd.) A. K. Mmieh,   Paul Adu-Gyamfi Esq
(National President)   *(National Secretary)*

DOCUMENT 22

National Union of Ghana Students Statement on the Transitional Provisions of the Constitution

The National Union of Ghana Students has received with shock the agreement between the Consultative Assembly and the government to indemnify all PNDC members and their appointees via the Transitional Provisions in the Constitution. These provisions which seek to protect all members of the PNDC and their appointees from any official act or omission have surely betrayed the startling hypocrisy of the high priests of probity and accountability. It is most incongruous that after a decade of probity and accountability slogan chanting those who coined the slogan and enforced it with the gun should now attempt to escape the litmus test.

The NUGS condemns the connivance of the PNDC and the Consultative Assembly to entrench in the Constitution such Transitional Provisions as would allow the PNDC and her cohort of appointees to go unquestioned about their performance. That the Consultative Assembly could pass such pertinent provisions without the usual debate makes of it a rubber stamp of which the NUGS could never have been a party.

Certainly, it is necessary to make provision for the orderly transfer of power and authority from the dictatorship of the military to a Constitutional and democratic government. But such provisions should be purely transitional and should not be tailored to seal forever the atrocities of human rights violations and criminal acts of either individuals in government or the government as a collective body.

It is a paragon of bunkums for the PNDC to have convicted and punished innocent Ghanaians since 1981 through its own kangaroo court viz. the Citizens Vetting Committee only to turn round to indemnify itself against the due process of justice. Is it not ironic to extend the indemnity to the coup plotters of 1966 and 1972 when their leading members have already been killed by the incumbency? Of better profit to them would have been for the PNDC to wish them "rest in peace".

The history of the AFRC, the Transitional Provisions in the 1979 Constitution and the subsequent overthrow of the Third Republic is enough warning to almost all Ghanaians that Transitional Provisions as prescribed by the PNDC are fraught with dynamos for political instability in the coming Fourth (4th) Republic.

Surely indemnity for coup plotters would be a morale booster for others of their ilks to commit the highest treason ever known of overthrowing popularly elected regimes and the law (Constitution) of the land. That makes it even more unfortunate for the Consultative Assembly to have passed these primitive provisions without any debate after having earlier spent time and effort on the methodologies of coup prevention.

In any case the Transitional Provisions, to the NUGS, are the last kicks of a dying horse for a hopeless survival.

We therefore call on all well-meaning Ghanaians to employ their newly earned culture of expression to stand up against these last antics of the macabre dance.

Issued By the National Executive Committee of the NUGS on the 31st March 1992.

(Sgd.) Samwin John Banienuba
(National Secretary)

DOCUMENT 23

GHANA BAR ASSOCIATION

Statement by the Ghana Bar Association on the Draft Constitution of the Republic of Ghana and the Proposed Referendum Thereon

At a Special General Meeting of the Ghana Bar Association held on Wednesday, 15 April, 1992, at the auditorium of the Ghana School of Law, Accra, there was a general debate on the Draft Constitution of the Republic of Ghana presented to the Provisional National Defence Council by the Consultative Assembly on the 31st day of March, 1992, and subsequently published in the Ghana Gazette.

The Draft Constitution and its Transitional Provisions

The consensus of opinion of members of the Ghana Bar Association is that the Draft Constitution of the Republic of Ghana has many points to commend it but that these good points are, unfortunately, overshadowed by certain sections of the transitional provisions and in particular by sections 34, 35 and 37 of the provisions. The Association unanimously rejected as totally undesirable and subversive of the major premise on which the Draft Constitution is based the said sections 34, 35 and 37 of the transitional provisions.

As regards sub-section (2) of section 34 of the transitional provisions, the Association notes that this subsection, with a few variations, is substantially similar to subsection (3) of section 13 of the transitional provisions to the 1969 Constitution but that no provisions in the 1969 Constitution are identical with subsections (1), (3), (4) and (5) of the said section 34 of the transitional provisions to the present draft constitution.

With regard to the 1979 Constitution, the Ghana Bar Association notes that subsections (2), (3), (4) and (5) of the transitional provisions to the Draft Constitution of 1992 are broadly similar to subsections (1), (2), (3) and (4) of section 14 of the transitional provisions to the 1979 Constitution, and that, to this extent, the 1979 Constitution went further than the 1969 Constitution in granting a blanket immunity from accountability by holders of public office during the period of rule of the military government in power immediately before the promulgation of the relevant constitution.

The Ghana Bar Association is firmly of the view that having regard to the history of this country since the coming into force of the 1979 Constitution, and having regard especially to the events that took place in this country following the overthrow of the Limann administration on the 31st day of December, 1981, provisions of the nature contained in subsections (1), (3), (4) and (5) of section 34 and in section 37 of the transitional provisions of the present Draft Constitution have no place in a democratic constitution erected on the twin pillars of probity and accountability on the part of public officers. Accordingly, the Ghana Bar Association totally rejects subsections (1), (3), (4) and (5) of section 34 and section 37 of the transitional provisions to the Draft Constitution.

The Ghana Bar Association is firmly of the view that it is a fraud on the people of this country to have transitional provisions of the far-reaching nature contained in sections 34, 35 and 37 of the transitional provisions to the Draft Constitution presented to the members of the Consultative Assembly in the manner in which these were presented, providing no opportunity for a general debate on such provisions by the general body of the Consultative Assembly and by the Ghanaian public at large. The Ghana Bar Association would like to draw attention to the fact that the records show that the transitional provisions to the 1969 Constitution were debated at great length by the members of the Constituent Assembly that drafted that Constitution and were not rammed down the throats of the members of that Constituent Assembly as was practically the case with the transitional provisions to the present Draft Constitution.

The Referendum

The Ghana Bar Association would further like to draw attention to the fact that it has never ceased to be of the view that a constitution containing complex issues spread over some 200 pages as the present Draft Constitution, is unsuitable for a 'Yes' or 'No' vote at a referendum and that such a referendum is, for all practical purposes, a farcical exercise in ascertaining the wishes of the people concerned and consequently of no value whatsoever. However, the Association, having failed to persuade the Provisional National Defence Council to change its mind on this nevertheless considers that it has a duty to the people of Ghana to make comments on the manner in which the referendum is to be conducted.

The Association totally rejects the formulation of the question for determination at the referendum since the question, as formulated, really calls for one answer to two questions, namely, whether the voter approves of the constitution as a whole, unreasonable though such a question is, and secondly, whether the voter agrees that the constitution should come into force on the 7th day of January, 1993, instead of immediately. These are two separate ideas and it is possible to give a 'Yes' answer to the first while giving a 'No' answer to the second. To roll both questions into one question is, therefore, to prevent the people of Ghana from expressing effectively their views as to whether the Constitution should come into force from the moment of approval or whether its coming into force should be postponed for another 8 months after it has been approved.

Further, the Ghana Bar Association is of the view that to give constitutional and political legitimacy to the presidential and parliamentary elections which have been scheduled to take place in November and December 1992, such elections and the regulations to be promulgated in regard thereto should be held and issued under the new constitution and not under laws formulated or promulgated entirely upon the authority of the Provisional National Defence Council which itself is a totally un-elected body.

For these reasons the Ghana Bar Association rejects the question for answer at the referendum as presently formulated and is of the view that the constitution should come into force upon its approval at the referendum and thereafter steps should commence to be taken to implement its provisions and all laws should depend for their legitimacy on its provisions.

The Interim National Electoral Commission

The Ghana Bar Association notes that the decision that the Constitution should come into force on the 7th day of January, 1993, is contained in the pre-independence anniversary speech of the Chairman of the Provisional National Defence Council delivered on radio and television on 5 March, 1992. The Association would have thought that this decision would not be incorporated into the question to be answered at the referendum and that such question would be formulated by the Interim National Electoral Commission independently of the government. That this was not done, is a matter for concern to the Ghana Bar Association with regard to the total independence of the government of the Interim National Electoral Commission, and the Ghana Bar Association conse--quently calls upon the Interim National Electoral Commission to demonstrate on every occasion its total independence of, and autonomy from, the Provisional National Defence Council and its agencies.

Oversight of the Transition to Democratic Rule

The Ghana Bar Association finds it totally unacceptable and intolerable a situation in which the Provisional National Defence Council undertakes political campaigning round the country at a time when there is a ban on party political activity and supervises and oversees the transition to democratic constitutional rule when all the indications are that the Provisional National Defence Council itself, or some prominent members thereof, intend to offer themselves for election and to take power under the constitution and to benefit from the various procedures that they have set in train. The Bar Association is of the view that such steps, to be impartially executed, should be taken and implemented only by an interim administration which has no interest in the steps that are being taken except the general interest of the country as a whole.

The Ghana Bar Association is of the view that if the Provisional National Defence Council should continue in power after the approval of the Draft Constitution, notwithstanding the objections strongly articulated in this and other statements of the Ghana Bar Association and by other well-meaning Ghanaians across the broad spectrum of political opinion in this country, then it should do so only in conformity with the provisions of the constitution as approved at the referendum and that all laws promulgated by it which are not in conformity with the provisions of the constitution should, for the avoidance of doubt and out of the abundance of caution, be expressly repealed or revoked.

Dated at Accra the 15th day of April, 1992
(Sgd.)   Anthony K. Mmieh,
         (National President)

DOCUMENT 24

Political Parties Law 1992
(PNDC Law 281) (Excerpts)

In pursuance of the Provisional National Defence Council (Establishment) Proclamation 1981, this Law is hereby made:

Part 1 — Registration of Political Parties

1. (1) Subject to the provisions of this Law, political parties may be founded in Ghana to further purposes which are not contrary to the laws of Ghana.
   (2) Subject to this law every citizen of Ghana of voting age has the right to form or join a political party
2. (1) No political party shall be formed —
   (a) on ethnic, regional, professional or religious basis; or
   (b) which uses words, slogans or symbols which could arouse ethnic, regional, professional or religious divisions.
   (2) For the purpose of subsection (1) of this section, a political party party is formed on ethnic, religious, regional or professional basis if its membership or leadership is restricted to members of any particular community, region, ethnic group, profession or religious faith or if its structure and mode of operation are not national in character.
3. (1) Every political party in Ghana shall be registered in accordance with the Law and shall pay in respect of the registration such fees as the Interim National Electoral Commission shall determine.
   (2) A fee payable under subsection (1) of this section is not refundable.
   (3) A political party registered under this Law shall be a body corporate and shall have perpetual succession and may sue and be sued in its corporate name.
4. The Interim National Electoral Commission hereafter referred to as "the Commission" shall register all political parties under this Law.
5. (1) No person shall —
   (1) canvass for votes; or
   (2) put forward a person for public election, on behalf of or

in the name of a political party unless the political party is registered under this Law.

(3) No political party shall organize or hold public meeting unless it has been issued with a final certificate of registration by the Commission under subsection (7) of section 8 of this Law.

6. (1) A political party shall not have as a leader of the party or a member of its executive a person who:
   (a) is not qualified to be elected as a member of Parliament under the Constitution approved at the Referendum held on 28th April 1992; or
   (b) is not qualified to hold public office; or
   (c) has not complied with the provisions of the Public and Political Party Office Holders (Declaration of Assets and Eligibility) Law, 1992 (PNDCL 280).

   (2) No political party shall have a founding member of the party a person who:
   (a) is not qualified to be elected as a member of Parliament under the Constitution approved at the Referendum held on 28th April 1992; or
   (b) is not qualified to hold public office.

   (3) A political party shall not be registered under this Law unless it has on its national executive committee or secretariat a member ordinarily resident or registered as a voter in each region.

7. (1) Subject to the provisions of this Law every citizen of voting age has the right to participate in political activity intended to influence the composition and policies of the Government.

   (2) Any person who suppresses or attempts to suppress the lawful political activity of another person commits an offence and shall on summary conviction be liable to a minimum fine of ¢50,000 or to imprisonment for a term not exceeding two years or to both.

8. (1) An application to register a political party shall be made to the Commission and shall be accompanied with:
   (a) two copies of the constitution and rule or regulations if any, of the political party duly signed by the interim national chairman or leader and by the interim national or general secretary of the party.
   (b) a list of the full names and addresses of at least one founding member of the political party from each district and such other particulars as the Commission may reasonably require;
   (c) a full description of the identifying symbols, slogans, and

colours, if any, of the political party; and
(d) the registration fee specified in subsection (1) of section 3 of this Law.

(2) The Commission shall, not later than seven days after the receipt of the application, issue the political party with a provisional certificate of registration and shall cause a notice of the application to be published in the *Gazette* as soon as practicable after receiving it, inviting objections from any person concerning the name, aim, objects, constitution, rule, symbols, slogans or colours of the party.

(3) The Commission may in addition to inviting objections to the application under subsection (2) of the section, cause independent enquiries to be made so as to ascertain the truth or correctness of the particulars submitted with the application for registration.

(4) On expiration of thirty days after the date of the publication of the Gazette notice the Commission shall, if satisfied that all the provisions of this Law with respect to registration have been complied with, register the political party.

(5) Where within the thirty day period an objection has been brought to the notice of the Commission it shall not register the political party until the objection has been disposed of to the satisfaction of the Commission.

(6) If the Commission upholds the objection or if enquiries made under subsection (3) of this section disclose that any of the particulars submitted with the application for registration are false, the Commission shall refuse to register the political party and cancel the provisional certificate issued to the political party under subsection (2) of this section.

(7) The Commission upon registering a political party shall issue to that party a final certificate of registration which shall be evidence that the provisions of the Law with respect to registration have been complied with.

9. (1) The Commission shall not register a political party under this Law unless it is satisfied:
(a) that its constitution and any rules or regulations submitted to the Commission for registration conform to democratic principles as provided in the constitution approved at the Referendum held on 28 April 1992;
(b) that there is in each district of Ghana a founding member of the party who is ordinarily resident in the district or is a registered voter in the district;

(c) that the party has branches in all the regions of Ghana and is, in addition organized in not less than two-thirds of the districts in each region;

(d) that the party's name, emblem, colour, motto or any other symbol has no ethnic, regional, religious or other sectional connotation or gives the appearance that its activities are confined only to a part of Ghana;

(e) that the executive officers of the political party have been elected under the supervision of the Commission in accordance with section 17 of this Law;

(f) that it is not in breach of any of the provisions of this Law; and

(g) that the purpose of the prospective political party is lawful.

(2) The membership of the national executive committee of a political party shall reflect membership from all regions of Ghana.

10. (1) The political parties specified in the First Schedule to this Law shall remain proscribed notwithstanding the repeal of the Political Parties Decree, 1979 (SMCD 229).

(2) The political parties specified in the Second Schedule to this Law are hereby proscribed.

(3) No person shall undertake any activity or action aimed at reorganizing or bringing into being any of the parties.

(4) The Commission shall not register any political party:

(a) under a name that is proscribed;

(b) under a name the abbreviations of which are the same as those of a proscribed political party; or

(c) with symbol, slogan, colour or name that is so similar to those of a proscribed political party as to make reasonable persons come to the conclusion that it is the same as or a successor to a proscribed political party.

11. No political party shall submit to the Commission for the purpose of section 8 of this Law, any identifying symbol, slogan, colour or name which is the same as the symbol, slogan, colour or name:

(a) of any other existing political party; or

(b) of the Republic; or

(c) of a proscribed political party; or which so closely resembles the symbol, slogan, colour or name of another political party, the Republic or a proscribed political party as the case may be, as to be likely to deceive the members of the public.

12. (1) Any political party whose application for registration is refused

by the Commission under this Law, may at any time apply to the Commission for it to reconsider its decision not to register the political party.

(2) If within fourteen days after an application has been made to it under subsection (1) of this section, the Commission refuses or fails to register the political party, the party may appeal to the Court of Appeal against the decision of the Commission and the decision of the Court shall be final.

(3) The appeal shall be on notice to the Commission and such other persons as the Court of Appeal may direct.

DOCUMENT 25

GHANA BAR ASSOCIATION PRESS CONFERENCE

Need For a Transitional Government

On 11 May 1991, the Ghana Bar Association (GBA) at an emergency general meeting called upon the PNDC to hand over the administration of Government by 1 July 1991 to a neutral interim administration headed by His Lordship The Chief Justice. The Ghana Bar Association felt at that time and still feels that there is need now than ever before for a neutral interim or transitional government to take over the reins of government from the PNDC, supervise the impending Presidential and Parliamentary elections and finally hand over to the President-elect. The Ghana Bar Association has arrived at this decision bearing in mind and judging by the dictatorial attitude of the PNDC, that the PNDC can potentially influence the duties of the Interim National Electoral Commission (INEC) in the organization of these elections. Ghanaians recall the era of I. K. Acheampong's tactics and unwarranted pressure on the Electoral Commissioner in 1978 to manipulate the voting in the UNIGOV referendum. In this regard, the Ghana Bar Association feels that the PNDC Government is not better than the Acheampong Regime.

The Ghana Bar Association feels that even though the PNDC Chairman has so far failed or deliberately refused to declare his intention to seek election to the office of President of the Fourth Republic, all indications are that he would, at short notice, put up himself for such a position. Should this happen, the Chairman would have by his delaying tactics sprung an unwarranted surprise on other Presidential candidates.

Even the alacrity with which the Chairman and his wife have been addressing durbars all over the country has already put the Chairman at a great advantage over the other aspiring Presidential candidates. The feeling in the country that the Chairman's clandestinely-sponsored political party is the National Democratic Congress (NDC) is so widespread that the Chairman, with all the secret agents at the disposal of his Government, cannot justifiably be heard to say that he does not know of the existence of that feeling or rumour. The better opinion is that he is aware of it but cannot deny his link with that party just to announce sooner or later that he is its Presidential candidate. The Ghana Bar Association feels that in the circumstances, it would be more honourable for all, the PNDC and the country as a whole, that the PNDC hand over now to an interim government.

Presidential Commission

In view of the foregoing, the Ghana Bar Association feels that owing to the paucity of time between now and the Presidential elections in early November 1992, a small but effective Government, capable of administering the country till 7 January 1993, should replace the PNDC at once. The Ghana Bar Association believes that while it could be ideal to select members of such a Government from various identifiable groups, the size of the Interim Government could become rather unwieldy and such a Government may thereby become ineffective and disastrous. The Ghana Bar Association therefore recommends that a small-sized Government comprising three members who have been well tested in public life and at least comparatively well known to the public and not known to be either directly or indirectly connected with any of the known political parties, past or present, should be constituted. The Association cannot think of any better national personalities fitting the description given above than the three living retired Chief Justices of Ghana, namely Messrs Samuel Azu Crabbe, F. K. Apaloo and E. N. P. Sowah.

These men have worked together, have known one another for years and judging by their past experience in life, the Ghana Bar Association feels that they cannot easily allow any personal conflicts which might have existed amongst them before to blind and let them forget the higher call of service and dedication to which they would be called in the supreme interest of the state. The three men should form a Presidential Commission with the most senior as Chairman. Needless to say, the Commission is to exercise both executive and legislative powers of State and will stay in office until 7 January 1993.

Ministerial Functions

The Ghana Bar Association feels that owing to the limited time between now and the Presidential elections in early November 1992, it would not be expedient to allow the Presidential Commission to appoint its Ministers since the appointment of such Ministers is bound to attract very sharp public criticisms and outcry not only from the political parties but also from the public at large. The Presidential Commission is likely to waste time answering criticisms over the appointment of Ministers instead of devoting its whole attention to managing the shattered economy effectively in the interim, supervising impartially the activities of the various political parties with a view to ensuring a peaceful transitional period and generally administering the country to the best of their ability, albeit for a short while. The Ghana Bar Association is of the view that the

Commission should not be offered any chance for exercising patronage, parochial or otherwise. Accordingly, the Ghana Bar Association recommends that the Administrative Heads of each existing Ministry should be empowered to exercise Ministerial functions in addition to their existing administrative duties while the Commission can, in appropriate circumstances, replace serving officers either for misconduct or where public interest so demands. The Commission should, also in its discretion, be free to assign Ministerial responsibilities to specific members of the Commission should they feel it convenient and necessary to do so.

Fate of Revolutionary Organs

The Ghana Bar Association feels that all the revolutionary organs set up during the PNDC rule should be disbanded on the dissolution of the PNDC itself. The Ghana Bar Association however feels that it would not be in the best interest of the country to merely disband the paramilitary organizations such as the CDO and the Commandos without making alternative provisions for them. Accordingly, the Ghana Bar Association feels that those members of these organizations who are considered by all the known criteria to be suitable for absorption into the Armed Forces should be so absorbed and the rest be afforded other avenues and opportunities for resettlement and rehabilitation.

Amnesty

7. The Ghana Bar Association is of the view that if the PNDC Government would not grant a general amnesty before being replaced with a Transitional Government, it is recommended that the Transitional Government should as a matter of primary concern grant a general and unconditional amnesty to persons of the following categories:
    (a) Persons convicted of any crimes which could be rightly described as political crimes such as subversion, etc.
    (b) Fugitives being persons wanted by the PNDC for trial for political crimes such as subversion.
    (c) Political exiles, voluntary or otherwise.
    (d) The eight (8) persons whose citizenship has been taken away by the PNDC in connection with the CIA spying episode in Ghana.

This recommendation is made in the spirit of reconciliation for the proper take-off of the Fourth Republic.

The Soussoudis Episode

8. It is the view of the Ghana Bar Association that the Soussoudis affair should not be left untouched. We do not however think that any useful purpose will be served by asking the Police to investigate this matter, but the better opinion is that a high-powered Commission of Enquiry comprising a retired Judge as Chairman, a retired Officer of the Ghana Armed Forces and a retired Police Officer be appointed to investigate the entire Soussoudis episode and make recommendations to Government.

Repressive Laws

The Ghana Bar Association is of the firm view that the existence of repressive laws in our statute books would undermine that atmosphere of freedom which is necessary and indispensable for the holding of free and fair elections and accordingly calls for the repeal of such laws.

Dated at the National Secretariat, Accra, this 20th day of August 1992.

(Sgd.) Anthony K. Mmieh,
(National President)

(Sgd.) Paul Adu-Gyamfi
(National Secretary)

DOCUMENT 26

GHANA BAR ASSOCIATION

1991/92 Annual Conference Held at Sekondi/Takoradi from 5 to 8 October, 1992

Part II

RESOLUTION NO 16/1992
REGISTER OF VOTERS

The Ghana Bar Association having examined the issues concerning the Electoral Register and appreciating that the population of Ghana is said to be 15.5 million, out of which more than half are under the age of 15 considers it fraudulent that the Electoral Register should contain 8.2 million registered voters.

Accepting the recommendation of the international team that examined the Electoral Register which recommended that for a free and fair election there was the need to compile a fresh Register of Voters.

Noting the Interim National Electoral Commission's purported cleaning of the said Register and its allegation that over one million dead or doubly registered persons have been removed from the said Register.

Taking note of the publication of Saturday 3 October, 1992 issue of the *Weekly Spectator* where in it was alleged that the final list of Registered Voters was 8.4 million which figure is higher than the figure prior to its so-called cleaning.

Resolves that no process of cleaning the said register can produce an honest, genuine and reliable Register for the conduct of free and fair elections; and hereby calls upon the Interim National Electoral Commission and the Government to commence forthwith the process of compiling a NEW Register of all eligible voters before the holding of the elections for the Fourth Republic even if this requires an adjustment in the scheduled date for ushering in the Government of the Fourth Republic; and That as a matter of urgency identity cards be issued to every eligible voter alongside the Registration process.

Dated this 8th day of October, 1992.

(Sgd.) Anthony K. Mmieh (Sgd.) Paul Adu-Gyamfi
(National President) *(National Secretary)*

DOCUMENT 27

GHANA BAR ASSOCIATION

1991/1992 Annual Conference Held at Sekondi/Takoradi from 5 October to 8 October 1992

PART III

RESOLUTION NO. 17 /1992

MATTERS AFFECTING THE NATION

WHEREAS

The Ghana Bar Association is desirous of ensuring a peaceful transition from over ten years of military dictatorship to constitutional democratic civilian rule and have persistently called upon the PNDC government to take certain fundamental steps to ensure the realization of such objectives in the supreme interest of the people of Ghana; and the Ghana Bar Association having observed that the PNDC government has deliberately refused to respond to such requests; and

The Ghana Bar Association is truly committed to ensure that:
(a) No further dirty tricks are employed to manipulate the presidential and parliamentary elections in the transitional process;
(b) The electoral process which is employed is free and fair;
(c) Political parties and their leaders are not intimidated or otherwise threatened or inhibited in any way during the electioneering campaign by the existence of obnoxious and pernicious laws;
(d) True reconciliation is promoted, in the political and social life of this country;

DO HEREBY RESOLVE AS FOLLOWS:

(i) *Interim Administration*
    (a) That in as much as the Chairman of the PNDC Mr. J. J. Rawlings, PNDC members, PNDC Secretaries, including PNDC Regional and District Secretaries and other PNDC appointees have openly participated in, sponsored, and supported the National Democratic Congress, a registered political party, which is vying for

political power with other registered political parties in the current public elections scheduled for November and December 1992 and in order to allay or remove any suspicion in the minds of the people of Ghana about the likelihood or interference with and manipulation of the electoral process, the Ghana Bar Association calls upon the said persons to step down immediately from their respective offices.

(b) That an Interim Administration comprising the three former Chief Justices of Ghana namely Messrs Honourable Justices Samuel Azu Crabbe, F. K. Apaloo and E. N. P. Sowah be appointed as a three-member Presidential Commission with the most senior as Chairman to supervise the forthcoming Presidential and Parliamentary elections and ensure a peaceful transition and hand over to the civilian elected President. If any of the said former Chief Justices shall be incapable of acting, his place must be filled by a respectable retired Justice of the Supreme Court to be nominated by the continuing members of the Commission.

(c) That during the transition the current administrative heads of existing ministries should be empowered to exercise Ministerial functions in addition to their existing administrative dutie

(ii) *Repressive Laws*

That the recent enactment of the Public Order (no. 2) Law which is a purported substitute for the repealed laws 4 and 91 should be condemned notwithstanding the power of review reserved thereunder in as much as it is a violation of the 1992 Constitution and the African Charter on Human and Peoples Rights to which our country is a signatory as there is the likelihood that it can be used to harass political opponents.

(iii) *Amnesty*

That an unconditional amnesty be granted to:
(a) Persons convicted of any crimes of political nature such as subversion.
(b) Fugitives being persons wanted by the PNDC for trial for alleged crimes of political nature.
(c) Political exiles, voluntary or otherwise.
(d) The eight Ghanians whose citizenship has been taken away by the PNDC in connection with the alleged CIA spying episode in Ghana (The Soussoudis Affair No.1).

(iv) *The Soussoudis Arms Haul Affair (No.2)*

That the discovery of a large cache of arms at the residence of Michael Soussoudis a cousin of Mr J. J. Rawlings should be probed immediately by a high-powered Commission of Enquiry comprising:

(a) A respectable retired Justice of the Superior Court of Judicature as Chairman.
(b) A respectable retired senior officer of the Ghana Armed Forces.
(c) A respectable retired senior officer of the Police Service.

(v) *Disbanding Revolutionary Organs*

That all the revolutionary organs of the PNDC Government should be disbanded and the competent and eligible persons among them may where appropriate be absorbed into the Security forces and the rest of them should be satisfactorily resettled.

(vi) *Interim National Electoral Commission*

That the Interim National Electoral Commission should be empowered to effectively supervise and control the activities of the political parties, check any interference in the conduct of free and fair Presidential and Parliamentary elections.

(vii) *Divestiture*

That the Ghana Bar Association whilst not opposed to the policy of the PNDC on the divestiture of Government Interest in Enterprises Programme, however deplores the mode of implementation of the said policy, and in particular our natural resources and the extractive industries such as our gold mines and our diamond industry to foreign investors under questionable circumstances on the eve of their handing over to a democratic constitutional civilian government which could conveniently have been floated as public companies in which Ghanaians could have been encouraged to invest.

(viii) *Probity and Accountability*

The Ghana Bar Association regrets that in spite of PNDC's crusading zeal on probity and accountability since they seized power more than ten years ago and prior to PNDC's assumption of office its Chairman was the Head of the AFRC which executed three former Heads of State in addition to other serving members of the then Government of SMC II on the principle of probity and accountability and went further to establish the June 4 Movement as reminder of the above principle; nevertheless the said PNDC has refused to account to the people of Ghana

for its stewardship namely:
- (a) refused to publish particulars of all loans contracted for and on behalf of the people of Ghana.
- (b) contracts and commitments made on behalf of the people of Ghana.
- (c) publication of salaries, wages and other emoluments paid to its members and other appointees.
- (d) publication of income and expenditure including defence expenditure, expenses on CDOs, CDRs and the Commandos and other so called revolutionary organs.

(ix) The Ghana Bar Association deplores the behaviour of the Chairman of the PNDC Mr J. J. Rawlings and his wife Nana Konadu Agyeman Rawlings in using intemperate and abusive language in calling political opponents as "fools and thieves" and "jokers" and calls upon him, his wife and followers to exercise the decorum that is expected of the holders of High Office and position.

(x) The Ghana Bar Association urges all Political Parties involved in the current electioneering campaign to exercise restraint and refrain from the use of provocative and abusive words and invectives.

Dated this 8th day of October, 1992

(Sgd.) Anthony K. Mmieh (Sgd.) Paul Adu-Gyamfi
(National President) *(National Secretary)*

DOCUMENT 28

THE CHRISTIAN COUNCIL OF GHANA

A Memorandum from the Christian Council of Ghana and the Catholic Church to the Interim Electoral Commission

On behalf of the Heads of Member Churches of the Christian Council of Ghana and the Catholic Bishops' Conference, we the Chief Executives of the two Secretariats jointly greet you in the precious name of our Lord and Saviour Jesus Christ.

We have followed with keen interest the evolving political process which will usher in the Fourth Republic of Ghana.

We are grateful to the Almighty God that since the PNDC Government and the people of Ghana embarked on the process of transition to constitutional democratic rule a few months ago, the exercise has been characterized by peace, harmony and a high sense of understanding among all the political forces in the country.

With the approval of the draft Constitution by the people of this country and the lifting of the ban on party political activities we have reached a crucial stage in the process where we should all get ourselves ready to elect those who will be in Government when the Fourth Republic of Ghana is inaugurated in January, 1993.

At this stage we believe that we are duty bound, as leaders of the Christian Community in this country, and in accordance with our prophetic role to draw your attention as the body set up to ensure smooth and fair elections, to a number of issues relevant to the current political and constitutional development in our country.

We are aware that elections are essential processes for establishing democratic representative governments. In a democracy, the authority of the government derives solely from the consent of the governed. The principal mechanism for translating that consent into governmental authority is the holding of free and fair elections. We are also aware that democracy thrives on openness and accountability with one very important exception, the act of voting itself.

By the decision of 28 April in which the majority of our people voted "YES" in favour of the draft Constitution, it follows that the die was cast for the return to constitutional rule. The conception that should give birth to the Fourth Republic took place on that day. What is required now is to ensure that the gestation period is not unduly disrupted, so that a healthy baby can be born to all of us.

This requires that we must all play the game fairly in the expectation of the birth of the Fourth Republic. This implies further, that from now on we must do things consistent with the provisions of the approved Constitution so that Ghana, reborn, should mature and grow in grace to its fullest possible stature. Fortunately, we realize that the electoral provisions in the approved Constitution are adequate for our purpose, providing for the independence of the Commission, that is to act as an organizer and referee of this game of party politics for election purposes. The provisions in the Constitution make room for the Electoral Commission to establish rules and regulations to ensure fair and responsible elections. We urge you in the name of God and of the people of this country, to boldly assume this responsibility under the approved Constitution as provided for in Articles 45, 46 and 51 which we quote [ ]

45. The Electoral Commission shall have the following functions:
    (a) to compile the register of voters and revise it at such periods as may be determined by law;
    (b) to demarcate the electoral boundaries for both national and local government elections;
    (c) to conduct and supervise all public elections and referenda;
    (d) to educate the people on the electoral process and its purpose;
    (e) to undertake programmes for the expansion of the registration of voters; and
    (f) to perform such other functions as may be prescribed by law.

46. Except as provided in this Constitution or in any other law not in consistent (sic) with this Constitution, in the performance of its functions, the Electoral Commission, shall not be subject to the direction or control of any person or authority.

51. The Electoral Commission shall, by constitutional instrument, make regulations for the effective performance of its functions under this Constitution or any other law, and in particular, for the registration of voters, the conduct of public elections and referenda, including provisions for voting by proxy.

We recognize that keeping and maintaining the independence of the Electoral Commission as provided for by the approved Constitution is essential in ensuring confidence in the elections and the electoral process! The PNDC Government after constituting the Interim National

Electoral Commission should understand that it has no right any more to interfere with its activities, but to allow it have a total independence in order to have the national and international confidence. Any interference should be vigorously resisted. Should resistance to pressures from any quarters yield no desired results, the members of the Commission should be bold enough to resign.

We urge your Commission to take on your constitutional responsibilities to set out the rules of the game and to make these known to all as soon as possible. Further, we would like to assure you of our prayers and support so that you can maintain your independence to ensure smooth and orderly transition into the Fourth Republic.

May the Grace of our Lord Jesus Christ be multiplied unto you, and may the Holy Spirit guide and sustain you so that you will be able to discharge your duties without fear or favour and to the glory of God.

(Sgd.) Rev. Fr. A.D. Balee
(Secretary General)
National Catholic Secretariat

Rev. David A. Dartey
(General Secretary)
Christian Council of Ghana   *17 June 1992*

DOCUMENT 29

The National Union of Ghana Students (NUGS) Resolution Declaring a Boycott of the 29 December Parliamentary Elections

The National Union of Ghana Students, having consistently and carefully monitored developments related to the transitional process to constitutional rule from 1990 to date:

Considering the fact that students of Ghana voted for a Fourth Republican constitution to return the country to a democratic multi-party constitutional rule and not a one party dictatorship:

Aware that the participating parties in the 29 December parliamentary elections constitute the "progressive alliance" of NDC, NCP and Egle Party with one presidential candidate and common convictions and therefore constitute one party:

Convinced that the said parliamentary elections will lead this country to a one party dictatorship which is in conflict with the spirit and letter of the Fourth Republican constitution:

Noting with dismay the contempt with which the government of the PNDC has treated our demand for a new voters' register, citizens' identity cards, a reconstituted Interim National Electoral Commission (INEC), general amnesty for political exiles, disbandment of all paramilitary organizations, repeal of all obnoxious laws and respect for the rights of political opponents as *sine-qua-non* for free and fair elections to democratic rule: and

Guided by our avowed pledge to remain faithful and loyal to Ghana our motherland:

Do hereby resolve:

1. that we as students of Ghana will not be part of any conscious and subtle attempt to return this country to a one party dictatorship;
2. that we students of Ghana declare a general boycott of the 29 December parliamentary elections;
3. that we shall participate in the elections when the appropriate structures to ensure free and fair elections are put in place.

Issued by the National Executive Committee for and on Behalf of Students of Ghana on 26 December 1992.

(*Sgd.*) Paul Asare Ansah
(National President)

George Sarpong
(National Secretary)

John Maxwell Mbeele
(National Treasurer)

John Qudjoe Kamassah
(Editor-in-Chief)

DOCUMENT 30

GHANA BAR ASSOCIATION

Statement by Ghana Bar Association on the Promulgation of the Constitution of the Fourth Republic

Since its inception, and most particularly during the last decade, the Ghana Bar Association has consistently championed in the Ghanaian polity the cause of democratic government, based on respect for the rule of law and fundamental human rights. The Bar it was, that stated in the very first year of the "revolution" its disapproval of the unconstitutional overthrow of the government of the duly elected President of the Third Republic, Dr Hilla Limann, and advocated that the PNDC should take rapid steps to return the country to constitutional, democratic government. The position of the Bar did not change during the entire period of PNDC rule. It led to the Bar being, in the early years of the "revolution", among the few leading voices in the wilderness protesting the atrocities and systematic violations of human rights that characterized the establishment of the regime of the PNDC, headed by Jerry John Rawlings, its Chairman.

The mindless kidnapping and brutal murder of the three judges of the High Court, whose only "crime" was their attachment to the rule of law, served to fortify the Bar's deeply-held conviction that the only civilized form of government for this nation of enormous potential was one which was founded on respect for the rule of law and fundamental human rights.

The unwavering, principled stance of the Bar began to attract more and more adherents, as the full horror of PNDC rule — kidnapping, murders, arbitrary arrests and detention of citizens, torture and mysterious deaths in state custody, unfolded. The Trades Union Congress (TUC), the National Union of Ghana Students (NUGS), the Churches, and eventually the Movement for Freedom and Justice (MFJ) joined the Bar to press the PNDC for a return to civilian government, based on democratic accountability in an open, free society. Eventually this pressure, in conjunction with external events that exposed the bankruptcy of authoritarian models of government such as existed in the former Soviet Union and East Germany, which inspired the "revolutionaries" of 31 December, 1981, bore fruit, and the PNDC reluctantly and belatedly became "converted" to the idea of democracy and constitutional government.

The global triumph of democracy over totalitarianism caught the PNDC regime unawares, and laid bare the ideological shallowness of many of its stated goals. With some trepidation, the PNDC then set in motion a series of measures that led to the promulgation of the Constitution and the inauguration of the Fourth Republic, a republic governed according to a constitution, which guarantees fundamental human rights and the independence of the judiciary, in short, the rule of law.

Unhappily for the nation, the coming into force of the Constitution was attended by disturbing events, the most significant of which was the perception by a segment of the population of the fraudulent nature of the 1992 presidential election, resulting in the boycott of the parliamentary elections by the main parties of the opposition. These events meant that the Fourth Republic began its life on a shaky foundation. The Bar, in the transitional period to the Fourth Republic, had, as was its wont, led the way in the nation-wide demand for equitable conditions in the democratic process — formation of a neutral, transitional government; replacement of the defective voters' register; repeal of all repressive laws; disarming of the paramilitary organs; grant of unconditional amnesty to all exiles; liberation of all political prisoners; establishment of a constituent, not consultative assembly. These demands of the Bar and of other like-minded bodies and individuals ring loudly through the papers of PNDC history. As the Bar rightly feared, the result of the PNDC's insensitivity to these demands is the present, troublesome climate of lack of confidence in the legitimacy of the institutions of the 4th Republic.

What, then, in these anxious moments of the nation's life, should be the attitude of the Ghana Bar Association? Surely our first concern, both as lawyers and as citizens, is to ensure that the Constitution, which enshrines respect for the rule of law and fundamental human rights, is fully observed. Governors and the governed should both obey the Constitution which the sovereign people of Ghana have chosen for their governance. That, then, is the first task of the Association — to preserve the constitutional order. The Constitution, especially as it relates to the indemnity provisions, remains a controversial document, but it does, nevertheless, address some of the most fundamental concerns of the Bar — respect for the rule of law and individual human rights. The Bar must endeavour to give meaning and effect to the Constitution as far as these are concerned. In this regard, the work of the Bar's National Human Rights Committee, and its regional chapters, will be an important indicator of the extent to which the Bar remains committed to its perennial ideals — the defence and promotion of the fundamental human rights of the people of Ghana.

It will be the aim of the Bar to make available to the ordinary citizen the full range of legal services, free of charge, which go to the protection and defence of the constitutionally-sanctioned rights of the individual. For too long, the individual Ghanaian's contact with the state has been characterized by arbitrariness and authoritarian attitudes, a situation that needs, in the current climate in Ghana and the world, to be radically reviewed and eliminated. The cause of individual rights and liberties must therefore remain the central goal of the Bar. That cause can only be realized if the independence of the judiciary is real and meaningful. A supine, sycophantic judiciary will pose the greatest obstacle to the realization of the Bar's central goal — that Ghana be a nation governed under God according to the rule of law. Thus, upholding the independence of the judiciary, and thereby ensuring its freedom from executive or other illegitimate interference, must form part of the Bar's central concerns. In this regard, the Bar extends to the judiciary the full hand of cooperation and friendship, and assures the judiciary that, in these testing times for the survival of the rule of law, the Bar will do its best to play its part in ensuring judicial independence and the rule of law.

The judiciary, for its part, bears an onerous responsibility in the preservation of the constitutional order, and thereby in guaranteeing the rule of law in Ghana. The Constitution has expressly conferred on the judiciary the exclusive power of interpretation and enforcement of the Constitution. The proper and effective use of this power will to a large extent determine the chances of survival of the Fourth Republic. The qualities required for the proper exercise of this power are self-evident — judicial integrity, and independence in the discharge of its constitutional obligations. A timorous judiciary, unable, where necessary, to control the acts of the executive or legislature, will undermine radically the chances of successful constitutional development. Our post-independence history, which provides several unfortunate examples of judicial timidity, illustrates the vital connection between judicial courage and the preservation of the rule of law and individual human rights. The Bar is hopeful that the judiciary will rise to the challenge of the times, and do its duty in accordance with the judicial oath which all judges take on their appointment.

Defence of the Constitution and the rule of law; upholding the independence of the judiciary; ensuring respect for fundamental human rights and liberties — these traditional objectives of the Bar need in the new constitutional order of the Fourth Republic to be restated and emphasized. The pursuit of these goals, however, will not blind the association to the wider struggle for social justice for the ordinary person in which the entire society is involved. The Bar will continue to speak out on all issues it considers germane to the good governance of the people of Ghana, which requires not only the enactment of just laws, but also the operation of efficient, equitable social services such as education, health and social welfare. The Bar expects in this regard that the executive will act in accordance with the letter and spirit of the Constitution. Consistent violations by the executive of the Constitution, about which already there is such anxiety, can only frustrate the desire of the overwhelming majority of Ghanaians for governance according to the rule of law, not the rule of man.

Parliament has been established by the Constitution to enact just laws, which will promote the ends of social harmony and social justice for all Ghanaians. The Bar intends vigorously to scrutinize the acts of both the executive and the legislature to ensure that the purposes of the Constitution are fully realized.

In undertaking these tasks, the Bar will continue to guard jealously its independence and its non-partisan nature. Even though the Bar contains in its membership all shades of political opinion, it has consistently refused to be partisan and to act as an ally of any political faction in the state. The Bar's actions are guided by its own openly declared goals and objectives as enshrined in its constitution. These principles will continue to govern its conduct. It is clear from the history of the last decade of PNDC rule that the existence of an independent, vigorous Bar, free to express its views on crucial national issues, is vital to the success of civilian government in Ghana. The Bar remains a powerful bulwark for the defence of civilized norms and values, and an implacable enemy of authoritarian government, which violates the human rights of the Ghanaian people. It is the solemn pledge of this generation of leaders and members of the Bar to maintain, preserve, and enrich this noble tradition, which has been forged and developed by past generations of lawyers, who were concerned about the public interest and the healthy development of the nation. Their shining example will be the yardstick by which the qualities of this generation of lawyers will be measured. With God's guidance and blessing, the Bar will not fail the nation.

Dated at Accra, this 13th day of March 1993

(*Sgd.*) Nutifafa Kuenyehia, Esq
(*National President*)

Paul Adu-Gyamfi, Esq
(*National Secretary*)

APPENDIX

Selected Documents Expressing the Political Position of the Ghana Trades Union Congress During the Late 1980s

DOCUMENT A

"The Trade Unions and Democracy in Ghana"

Paper Presented to the National Commission on Democracy by the Trades Union Congress

Topic: "The Trades Unions and Democracy in Ghana"

We present these views as perspectives on the question of democracy that provides the framework and conditions for the exercise of the authority of the people in government and affairs of the nation. In presenting these views, we make the preliminary observation that the whole approach to the question of democracy as adopted by the NCD is indeed diversionary and seeks to direct us to look for democracy in mere *forms* of government, whereas the essence of *democracy* lies in the creation and existence of political economic conditions that promote the overall material and cultural well-being of the people. We make this observation more so because especially at a time when the country is supposed to be "searching for democracy", *undemocratic* policies that impose heavy socio-economic burdens on large sections of the population are being pursued by government.

In these circumstances, it is difficult for us to reconcile a "search for democracy" with measures that undermine and erode democratic rights and gains of the people. In this connection, we cite the situation of continuing fall in the living standards of the population, the persistent situation of wages that are out of proportion to the high prices of goods and services; the increasing cost burden of education and health care on the people as well as the rising water and electricity bills; the on-going retrenchment that is increasing the level of unemployment among the population; the intermittent attacks on the labour movement and the growing assaults on trade union rights, the developing pattern of harassment and intimidation of militant workers and other democratic minded individuals.

In the light of the foregoing we note as follows:

1. That genuine democracy for us shall mean the organization of society in such a manner that the interests of the majority prevail.
2. That social groups and classes with opposing interests exist in Ghana and that therefore it is erroneous to think that all social groups and classes and their interests can be reconciled for a political system favourable to *all* to be evolved;
3. That democracy that serves and promotes the interests of the people necessarily undermines the interests of the minority exploiting and parasitic social groups and classes. For genuine democracy that caters for the interests of the people, *the people* refers to the vast majority of *workers, peasants,* fisherfolk, large numbers of small self-employed like traders, artisans, technicians, etc., intellectuals, soldiers, policemen and other professionals as well as national industrialists who are committed to social justice.
4. That the political power of the exploiting classes and neo-colonialist social forces are concentrated in the civil service bureaucracy; the judicial system and legal regime, the police, security agencies, army, educational system, the state-owned mass media, all of which make up the state machinery and have their origin in colonialism and therefore bear the stamp of foreign interests and an authoritarian culture. As the central pillar of political power that is essentially wielded to further the interests of the minority economically powerful social classes, and which political power is primarily responsible for the administration of modern Ghanaian society to the detriment of the masses, this state machinery must be completely dismantled in the long run and in its place developed alternative state institutions that are subject to the democratic authority of the people;
5. That the problems of genuine democracy for the people today arise from socio-economic and political relations that are rooted in colonialism and neo-colonialism. The resolution of these problems lies in the organization, mobilization and consistent struggle of the exploited and oppressed classes, i.e. the people, for the overthrow of neo-colonialism and the establishment of a new social order;
6. That the question of democracy for the masses relates to the political framework and conditions under which they can work out their emancipation from the exploitation and authoritarian political rule of the minority economically powerful social groups and classes. That this is not merely a question of working out some "model", home-grown

form of government, but rather that of ensuring the political power and rule of the masses as the primary issue. The form which this ultimately takes will be decided by the people, for when the democratic majority wield power through struggle, there will be no question about what form of government to institute; the people themselves will establish, free from any restrictions of the old order, their own democratic form of government that will nonetheless be on the basis of a highly disciplined and ordered society, but a discipline and order of a radically new character.

7. That this demands above all that the political power of the exploiting classes and the institutions through which this is exercised (Ref. paragraph 4) must be replaced by the power of the exploited classes and social groups organized to defend and promote their social, economic and political interests. This depends fundamentally on strengthening the masses in their independent organizations and providing room for their views to affect national policy formulation and implementation. That this is the context in which the TUC is today calling on the PNDC to take immediate steps to establish a popularly and democratically constituted People's Assembly as a transitional organ to be responsible for the overall determination and assessment of Government policy and implementation, as well as supervise the general operation of various public institutions, namely the civil service, the mass media, the legal system, the defence and security agencies, public corporations, etc. and also to vet appointments to high state office. This Assembly is to be made up essentially of the elected representatives of the mass organizations of the people. That for us the PNDC's readiness to work for the establishment of this democratic Assembly that oversees national policy, Governmental practice and the performance of state institutions will be a test of its practical commitment to promote democracy for the masses.

8. That to demonstrate its commitment to genuine democracy for the people, the PNDC must encourage the independent organization, mobilization and struggle of the popular masses by creating favourable conditions for the free and unfettered expression of their views on all matters of concern to the nation. Thus, the state-owned mass media should give prominence to issues of concern to the masses as well as to the expression of their views. Besides, government should not interfere with the development of independent newspapers for the trade unions and other organizations of working people as well as for other democratic sections of the population like students and youth.

9. That the right of workers to undertake mass demonstration and to

withhold their labour must be recognized without police restrictions and intimidation.
10. That to help develop and foster a spirit of democratic self-confidence among the people, the right to education must be recognized by the state. Consequently, Government must commit resources to make education fee-free and compulsory as well as initiate a mass campaign to wipe out illiteracy among adults.
11. That it is our conviction that the people can actually be drawn into the debate on the political-economic future of the country by being encouraged and supported to strengthen their own independent mass and political organization and to struggle against all policies that are inimical to their interests.

Dated 17 December 1986.

DOCUMENT B

Extract from Secretary General's May Day Address, 1987

... [ ] The theme for this year's May Day, as already mentioned, is "Ghana in Search of Democracy". Society creates for itself, as the oyster its shell, an inner environment of customs, traditions and institutions within which it lives. The TUC takes this occasion to welcome the PNDC's announcement of its intention to hold district elections. Election of leaders is part of the institution of democracy which today is a permanent and fundamental concern in modern society. We believe, however, that the election of leaders at the district level must necessarily be linked to election of leaders at the national level and election of government by the people as a whole.

Again, contrary to the simple issue of guidelines for the election, it is our view that elections are so important that they must be held within the framework of a constitution for the nation.

The National Commission for Democracy must speedily present the results of its search to the nation so that a National Constituent Assembly can be democratically convened to formulate a constitution for the approval of the people of this country. The political traditions and aspirations of the people cry for democracy and it is the contention of organized labour that time is running out. The question of democratic government of the people by the people and for the people is high on the workers, agenda today.

As we in Ghana continue in our struggle for our rights and democratic system of government, we also extend our arms in combative solidarity with the workers and people of South Africa as they fight to overthrow the brutal system of apartheid, a system that today stands as an affront against the whole of mankind.

We also extend our solidarity to the struggling people of Namibia and renew the call for the imposition of mandatory economic sanctions against the racist regime of South Africa.

We take this occasion of the international day of solidarity for workers to express our solidarity with workers and other struggling people of the Middle East, Chile, Nicaragua, El Salvador and the rest of the world.

LONG LIVE INTERNATIONAL WORKERS SOLIDARITY!
LONG LIVE TUC!!

DOCUMENT C

Resolutions Adopted by the 3rd Quadrennial Delegates Congress of the Trade Union Congress (Ghana) Held at the University of Cape Coast from 16 to 18 March, 1988

Delegates from National affiliated to the Trades Union Congress (Ghana) meeting at its 3rd Quadrennial Delegates Congress deliberated on diverse issues, including, the situation of the National Economy, Political Situation, Education, Housing, Industrial Relations, International Affairs, etc. and finally adopted the following Resolutions:

1. Political Issues

(i) That the Trades Union stands committed to the fundamental right of the people to decide democratically on the political system of the nation and by whom they will be governed at all levels of the structures created by the political system. To secure this, Trades Union Congress sees the following steps as basic:
   (a) the drafting of a Constitution by representatives of groups or which can be considered representatives of the broad spectrum of the Ghanaian people, e.g. the Labour Movement, farmers and fishermen, security organizations, professionals;
   (b) the democratic discussion of the draft Constitution by the people;
   (c) convocation of a Assembly to finalize the draft Constitution and a timetable for the establishment of a government based on the adopted Constitution;
   (d) a national on the Constitution and the time table;
   (e) the time-frame for the processes indicated above should be two years.
(ii) That the TUC reaffirmsits position that election to government offices at all levels; i.e. from District to National, must be within the frame work of a National Constitution. Constitutional Rule is fundamental because:
   (a) a National Constitution will clearly indicate the relationship among all levels of government whether vertical, i.e. District

to National, or horizontal, i.e. Executive, Judiciary and Parliamentary;
  (b) in this connection, the TUC rejects the proposed District Level Elections based on the Blue Book, since they are not in consonance with the above stated case.
(iii) That the process of establishing a political system and government democratically decided by the people requires the recognition of fundamental democratic rights, namely:
  (a) the right to associate around common goals or views whether social, economic or political;
  (b) the right to free expression in various terms:
    — speech
    — assembly
    — writing, including newspapers;
  (c) abolition of detention without trial such as under PNDC Law 4 (Protective Custody Law) and the trial or release of all detainees;
  (d) an end to widespread arbitrariness of government officials, security personnel, etc.
(iv) That the Trade Union Movement accepts the Directive Principles of State Policy which were first contained in the 1979 Constitution of Ghana and are also laid out in PNDC Law 42 and calls for their inclusion in any future Constitution . . .